Editor
Lorin Klistoff, M.A

Managing Editor
Karen J. Goldfluss, M.S. Ed.

Illustrator
Teacher Created Resources Staff

Cover Artist
Brenda DiAntonis

Art Production Manager
Kevin Barnes

Art Coordinator
Renée Christine Yates

Imaging
Rosa C. See

Publisher
Mary D. Smith, M.S. Ed.

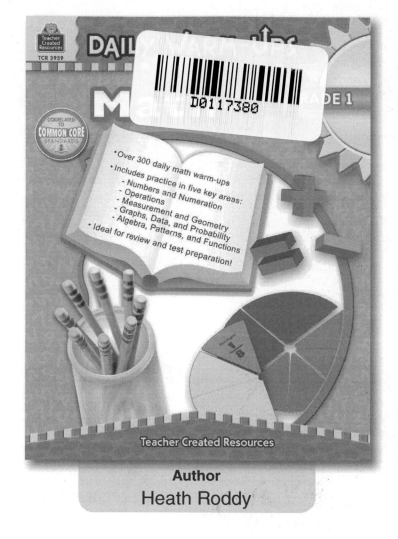

Author
Heath Roddy

Correlations to the Common Core
State Standards can be found at
http://www.teachercreated.com/standards/.

Teacher Created Resources, Inc.
6421 Industry Way
Westminster, CA 92683
www.teachercreated.com

ISBN: 978-1-4206-3959-9

©2006 Teacher Created Resources, Inc.
Reprinted, 2014
Made in U.S.A.

Gill's Academy 2
3965 Almaden Expressway #165
San Jose, CA 95120
408-323-8388

G711

Teacher Created Resources

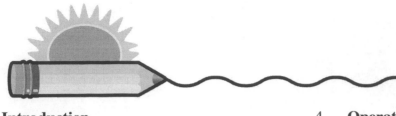

Table of Contents

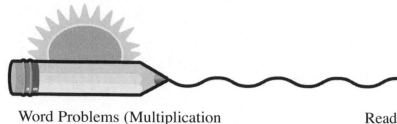

Table of Contents

Introduction

The *Daily Warm-Ups: Math* series was written to provide students with frequent opportunities to master and retain important math skills. The unique format used in this series provides students with the opportunity to improve their own fluency in math. Each section consists of at least 30 pages of challenging problems that meet national and state standards. (See Table of Contents to find a listing of specific subject areas.) Answer keys are located at the back of each section. Use the tracking sheet on page 6 to record which warm-up exercises you have given your students. Or, distribute copies of the sheet for students to keep their own records.

This book is divided into five sections. The sections are as follows:

- Numbers and Numeration
- Operations
- Measurement and Geometry
- Graphs, Data and Probability
- Algebra, Patterns and Functions

Daily Warm-Ups: Math gives students a year-long collection of challenging problems to reinforce key math skills taught in the classroom. As students become active learners in discovering mathematical relationships, they acquire a necessary understanding that improves their problem-solving skills and, therefore, boosts their confidence in math. When using this book, keep the idea of incorporating the warm-ups with the actual curriculum that you may be currently using in your classroom. This provides students with a greater chance of mastering the math skills.

This book can be used in a variety of ways. However, the exercises in this book were designed to be used as warm-ups in which students will have the opportunity to work problems and obtain immediate feedback from their teacher. To help ensure student success, spend a few moments each day discussing problems and solutions. This extra time will not take very long and will yield great results from students. As you use this book, you will be excited to watch your students discover how exciting math concepts can be!

Teaching Tips

Ideas on how to use the warm-ups are as follows:

- *Discussion*—Most warm-ups can be completed in a short amount of time. When time is up, model how to correctly work the problems. You may wish to have students correct their own work. Allow time for students to discuss problems and their solutions to problems. You may want to allow students the opportunity to discuss their answers or the way they solved the problems with partners. Discuss why some answers are correct and why others are not. Students should be able to support their choices. Having students understand that there are many ways of approaching a problem and strategies used in dealing with them are a great benefit for all students. The time you allow students to do this is just as important as the time spent completing the problems.

- *Review*—Give students the warm-up at the end of the lesson as a means of tying in an objective taught that day. The problems students encounter on each warm-up are designed to improve math fluency and are not intended to be included as a math grade. If the student has difficulty with an objective, then review the material again with him or her independently and provide additional instruction.

Introduction

Teaching Tips *(cont.)*

- *Assessment*—The warm-ups can be used as a preliminary assessment to find out what your students know. Use the assessment to tailor your lessons.

- *Introduction*—Use the warm-ups as an introduction into the new objective to be taught. Select warm-ups according to the specific skill or skills to be introduced. The warm-ups do not have to be distributed in any particular order.

- *Independent Work*—Photocopy the warm-up for students to work on independently.

- *Transparencies*—Make overhead transparencies for each lesson. Present each lesson as a means of introducing an objective not previously taught, or have students work off the transparency.

- *Model*—Invite students to come to the board to model how they approached a problem on the warm-up.

- *Test Preparation*—The warm-ups can be a great way to prepare for math tests in the classroom or for any standardized testing. You may wish to select warm-ups from all sections to use as practice tests and/or review prior to standardized testing.

Student Tips

Below is a chart that you may read to the students. Or, photocopy and cut out for each student's parents. It will give students a variety of strategies to use when dealing with difficult problems.

Math Tips

✓ Write word problems as number problems.

✓ Underline the question and circle any key words.

✓ Make educated guesses when you encounter multiple-choice problems or problems with which you are not familiar.

✓ Leave harder problems for last. Then, come back to solve those problems after you have completed all other problems on the warm-up.

✓ Use items or problem-solving strategies, such as drawing a diagram or making a table to solve the problem.

✓ Always check your answer to see that it makes sense.

Tracking Sheet

Numbers and Numeration Warm-Ups

1		8		15		22		29		36		43		50		57	
2		9		16		23		30		37		44		51		58	
3		10		17		24		31		38		45		52		59	
4		11		18		25		32		39		46		53		60	
5		12		19		26		33		40		47		54		61	
6		13		20		27		34		41		48		55		62	
7		14		21		28		35		42		49		56			

Operations Warm-Ups

1		8		15		22		29		36		43		50		57	
2		9		16		23		30		37		44		51		58	
3		10		17		24		31		38		45		52		59	
4		11		18		25		32		39		46		53		60	
5		12		19		26		33		40		47		54		61	
6		13		20		27		34		41		48		55		62	
7		14		21		28		35		42		49		56			

Measurement and Geometry Warm-Ups

1		8		15		22		29		36		43		50		57	
2		9		16		23		30		37		44		51		58	
3		10		17		24		31		38		45		52		59	
4		11		18		25		32		39		46		53		60	
5		12		19		26		33		40		47		54		61	
6		13		20		27		34		41		48		55		62	
7		14		21		28		35		42		49		56			

Graphs, Data and Probability Warm-Ups

1		8		15		22		29		36		43		50		57	
2		9		16		23		30		37		44		51		58	
3		10		17		24		31		38		45		52		59	
4		11		18		25		32		39		46		53		60	
5		12		19		26		33		40		47		54		61	
6		13		20		27		34		41		48		55		62	
7		14		21		28		35		42		49		56			

Algebra, Patterns and Functions Warm-Ups

1		8		15		22		29		36		43		50		57	
2		9		16		23		30		37		44		51		58	
3		10		17		24		31		38		45		52		59	
4		11		18		25		32		39		46		53		60	
5		12		19		26		33		40		47		54		61	
6		13		20		27		34		41		48		55		62	
7		14		21		28		35		42		49		56			

NUMBERS AND NUMERATION

Jumping Up Learning Circles
5965 Almaden Expy Suite 165
San Jose, CA95120
408-323-8388

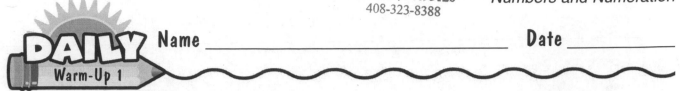

Numbers and Numeration

DAILY Warm-Up 1

Name _____   Date _____

1. Look at the calculator. If you add 7 to the total, what would the display read? (*Circle the correct letter.*)

A. 6   **C.** 19

B. 7   **D.** 20

2. Shannon has 23 pennies. Shade in the number of pennies Shannon has on the model to the right. (*Use your pencil.*)

Numbers and Numeration

DAILY Warm-Up 2

Name _____   Date _____

1. Write the number below in words.

Tens	Ones
1	8

_____

2. If you add 10 to the number below, what would the new number be? (*Write your answer on the line.*)

Tens	Ones
5	5

_____

Jumping Up Learning Circles
5965 Almaden Expy Suite 165
San Jose, CA95120
408-323-8388

Numbers and Numeration

Name _____ **Date** _____

1. How many hearts are shown below? (*Write your answer on the line.*)

_____

2. Which answer choice below is **true**? (*Circle the correct letter.*)

A. 29 > 35   **C.** 24 > 27

B. 43 < 43   **D.** 23 > 21

Numbers and Numeration

Name _____ **Date** _____

1. Which answer choice below is **false**?

A. 119 = one hundred nineteen   **C.** 410 = four hundred ten

B. 223 = two hundred twenty-six   **D.** 387 = three hundred eighty-seven

2. Look at the model below. How many **tens** are shown?

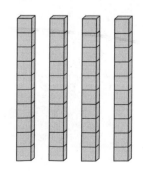

There are _____ tens.

Jumping Up Learning Circles
5965 Almaden Expy Suite 165
San Jose, CA 95120
408-323-8388

DAILY Warm-Up 5

Name _____ **Date** _____

1. How many marbles does Lee have? (*Write your answer on the line.*)

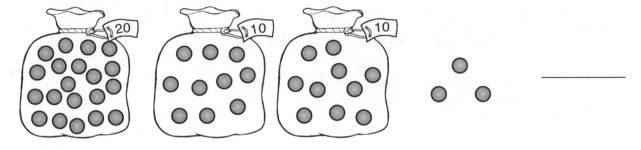

_____

2. Circle the **smaller** number.

97   94

DAILY Warm-Up 6

Name _____ **Date** _____

1. Write the numbers below.

A. twelve = _____   **C.** sixty-three = _____

B. twenty-seven = _____   **D.** twenty-two = _____

2. Circle the **even** numbers.

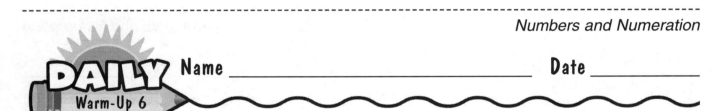

1   2   3   4   5   6   7   8   9

Jumping Up Learning Circles
5965 Almaden Expy Suite 165
San Jose, CA 95120
408-323-8388

DAILY Warm-Up 7

Numbers and Numeration

Name _____   Date _____

1. Look at the chart below. Complete the chart by adding the missing numbers.

23	24				28		30	31	32	33	
35		37		39	40	41					46
	48	49					54	55		57	
59		61	62		64	65		67			70

2. Draw a ring around the 4th shape.

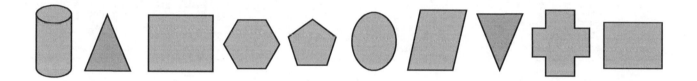

Numbers and Numeration

DAILY Warm-Up 8

Name _____   Date _____

1. How many bikes are shown below? Circle the correct answer, and then write the number in words.

A. 8   --
_____

B. 10 --
_____

C. 12 --

2. Write the number of spiders in each group.

_____   _____   _____

DAILY **Name** _____ **Date** _____
Warm-Up 9

1. Write the numbers to the picture problem below.

_____ + _____ = _____

2. Write how many seeds are in each apple on the spaces below in number form.

_____   _____   _____   _____
- - - - - - - - -   - - - - - - - - -   - - - - - - - - -   - - - - - - - - -
_____   _____   _____   _____

DAILY **Name** _____ **Date** _____
Warm-Up 10

1. Fill in the chart.

	Tens	Ones
14 =		
12 =		
33 =		

2. Look at the models below. Write the number of tens and ones, and then write the number in the spaces provided.

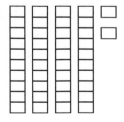 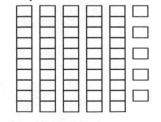 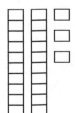

_____ tens _____ ones   _____ tens _____ ones   _____ tens _____ ones

number = _____   number = _____   number = _____

Name _____ **Date** _____

1. What number is **one less than 89**? (*Circle the correct letter.*)

   A. 90   **B.** 89   **C.** 88

2. Use your pencil to color numbers **greater than 25 but less than 35** on the block of numbers below.

1	2	3	4	5	6	7	8	9	10
11	12	13	14	15	16	17	18	19	20
21	22	23	24	25	26	27	28	29	30
31	32	33	34	35	36	37	38	39	40
41	42	43	44	45	46	47	48	49	50
51	52	53	54	55	56	57	58	59	60
61	62	63	64	65	66	67	68	69	70
71	72	73	74	75	76	77	78	79	80
81	82	83	84	85	86	87	88	89	90
91	92	93	94	95	96	97	98	99	100

Name _____ **Date** _____

1. Where should the number 30 go? (*Circle the correct letter.*)

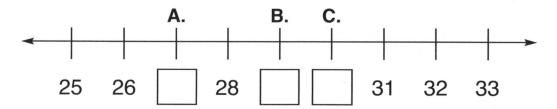

        A.   **B.**   **C.**

25   26   ☐   28   ☐   ☐   31   32   33

2. Look at the fraction below. Use your pencil to color $\frac{1}{2}$ of the rectangle.

$\frac{1}{2}$

Name _____ **Date** _____

1. Which object below costs the **most**? (*Circle the correct letter.*)

  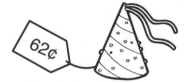

A. 57¢ B. 95¢ C. 62¢

2. Look at the numbers below. Circle the number that is **smaller** in each set.

A.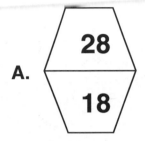
28
18

B.
35
53

C.
17
27

D.
37
27

Name _____ **Date** _____

Warm-Up 14

1. Look at the hundreds chart. Use the chart to find the mystery number.

- I am a number greater than 20 but less than 30.
- I am not an even number.
- I have two numbers that equal 9 when added together.

The mystery number is _____ .

1	2	3	4	5	6	7	8	9	10
11	12	13	14	15	16	17	18	19	20
21	22	23	24	25	26	27	28	29	30
31	32	33	34	35	36	37	38	39	40
41	42	43	44	45	46	47	48	49	50
51	52	53	54	55	56	57	58	59	60
61	62	63	64	65	66	67	68	69	70
71	72	73	74	75	76	77	78	79	80
81	82	83	84	85	86	87	88	89	90
91	92	93	94	95	96	97	98	99	100

2. How is the number **34** written?

A. thirteen

B. three four

C. thirty-four

D. forty-three

DAILY Warm-Up 15   Name _____ Date _____

1. Write the missing numbers.

14   15   16   19   20   21   22   23

_____ and _____

2. How much is shown below?

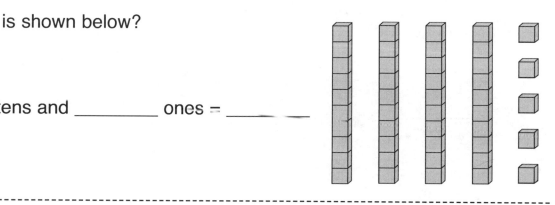

_____ tens and _____ ones = _____

- -

DAILY Warm-Up 16   Name _____ Date _____

1. Circle sets of tens below. Write the number of tens and ones. Then write the number.

_____ tens _____ ones = _____

2. Write the fractions.

A.

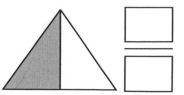

□ shaded parts

□ equal parts

B.

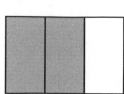

□
—
□

□ shaded parts

□ equal parts

Name _____   **Date** _____

1. Complete the chart by counting by **fives**.

5	10			25		35
40	45	50	55		65	70
75		85	90	95		105

2. Write the number for **eighteen**.

_____

Name _____   **Date** _____

1. Which number is **one more than twenty-six**? (*Circle the correct letter.*)

A. 27   **B.** 26   **C.** 25

2. Write these numbers in order from **largest to smallest**.

11	9	13	7	15	14

_____ _____ _____ _____ _____ _____

Jumping Up Learning Circles
5965 Almaden Expy Suite 165
San Jose, CA95120
408-323-8388

DAILY Warm-Up 19

Name _____   Date _____

1. Look at the pencils. Which group shows the pencils placed from **longest to shortest**? (*Circle the correct letter.*)

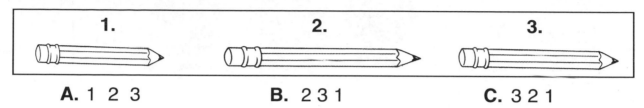

A. 1 2 3   **B.** 2 3 1   **C.** 3 2 1

2. Look at the numbers in the boxes. Write the numbers on the correct lines showing the greater value.

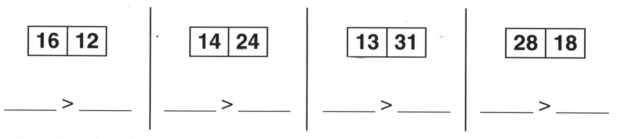

| 16 | 12 | | 14 | 24 | | 13 | 31 | | 28 | 18 |

_____ > _____ | _____ > _____ | _____ > _____ | _____ > _____

- -

DAILY Warm-Up 20

Name _____   Date _____

1. Draw a line from each number to its correct model.

4 tens 3 ones   **A.**

6 tens 0 ones   **B.**

8 tens 6 ones   **C.**

2. Write the number word.

9 _____

8 _____

5 _____

DAILY
Warm-Up 21

Name _____ Date _____

1. Is the **sixth** shirt black? *(Circle "Yes" or "No.")*

Yes   **No**

2. Draw a circle around the **even** numbers below.

0   1   2   3   4   5   6   7   8   9

DAILY
Warm-Up 22

Name _____ Date _____

1. Use your pencil to shade $\frac{1}{2}$ of the rectangles.

☐ ☐ ☐ ☐ ☐ ☐

2. Mary and Pete bought a dozen cookies. Did they each get an **equal** amount of the cookies? *(Circle "Yes" or "No.")*

Yes   **No**

Name _____ **Date** _____

1. How much is shown below? *(Write your answer on the line.)*

_____ cents

2. Count by fours and write the numbers.

_____   _____   _____   _____

Name _____ **Date** _____

1. Draw a ring around the **twelfth** lamp.

2. Look at the numbers below. Mark wrote a number with a 4 in the tens place and a 5 in the ones place. Circle the number Mark wrote, and then write the number word on the line below.

46	65	48	45	54

_____

DAILY
Warm-Up 25

Name _____   Date _____

1. How many keys are shown? Circle the correct letter, and then write the number word.

_____

A. 5 -

B. 6 -

C. 7 -

2. Color each fraction below.

Color $\frac{1}{2}$ green.   Color $\frac{1}{3}$ red.   Color $\frac{1}{4}$ orange.   Color $\frac{1}{2}$ green.

DAILY
Warm-Up 26

Name _____   Date _____

1. Which number is **one more than thirty-eight**? (*Circle the correct letter.*)

A. thirty-nine   **B.** forty-nine   **C.** thirty-seven

2. Which tally marks show **18**? (*Circle the correct letter.*)

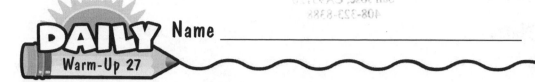

Name _____   **Date** _____

1. How much money is shown below? *(Write your answer on the line.)*

_____ cents

2. Write the word for each number.

7

_____
- -
_____

9

- -
_____

6

- -

Name _____   **Date** _____

1. Write the number that comes after each number below.

4, _____, 6, _____, 8, _____, 10, _____

2. Look at the tally marks. How much is shown? *(Circle the correct letter.)*

A. 23   **B.** 24   **C.** 25

Jumping Up Learning Circles
5965 Almaden Expy Suite 165
San Jose, CA95120
408-323-8388

Name _____

Date _____

Warm-Up 29

1. Color $\frac{1}{2}$ of the shirts with your pencil.

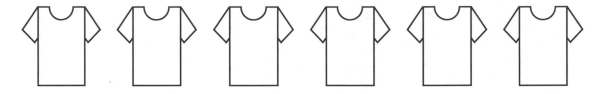

2. Color the **fifth** apple. Then write its number and word.

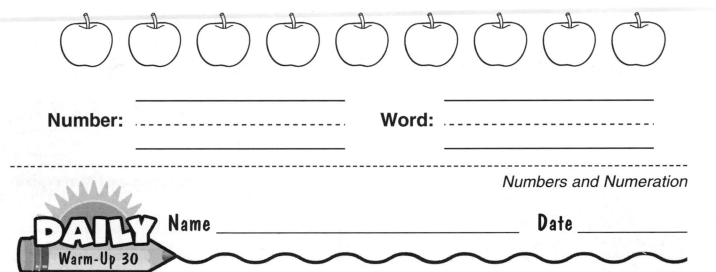

Number: ------------------------------   **Word:** ------------------------------

---

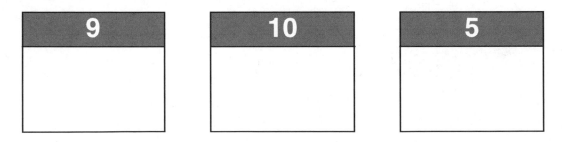

Name _____

Date _____

Warm-Up 30

1. Use tally marks to show each number.

9	10	5

2. How much is a **nickel** worth? *(Circle the correct letter.)*

A. 1 cent   **B.** 5 cents   **C.** 10 cents

Jumping Up Learning Circles
5965 Almaden Expy Suite 165
San Jose, CA95120
408-323-8388

DAILY

Warm-Up 31

Name _____ Date _____

1. Circle the letter of the **largest** value.

A. quarter   **B.** dime   **C.** nickel

2. Which answer shows **9 cents**? (*Circle the correct letter.*)

A. nickel,   penny,   penny,   penny

B. nickel,   penny,   dime

C. nickel,   penny,   penny,   penny,   penny

DAILY

Warm-Up 32

Name _____ Date _____

1. Color $\frac{1}{4}$ of the shape below.

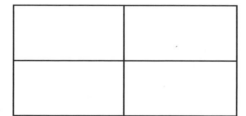

2. Which circle is divided into two **equal** parts? (*Circle the correct letter.*)

A.

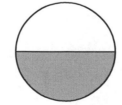
B.

C.

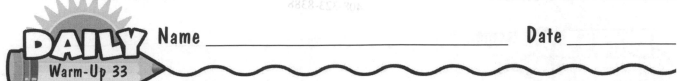

Name _____ **Date** _____

DAILY
Warm-Up 33

1. Look at the group of pencils. Which group has exactly **7 pencils**? (*Circle the correct letter.*)

A.   **B.**   **C.**

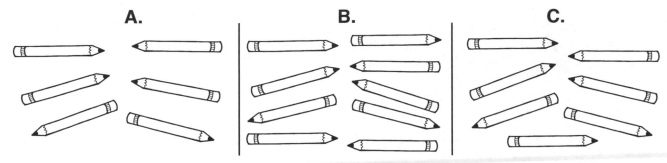

2. Use tally marks to show how many basketballs are shown below.

   _____

DAILY
Warm-Up 34

Name _____ **Date** _____

1. Circle "Yes" or "No" for each problem below.

9 > 5	5 > 9	9 = 9
Yes No	**Yes No**	**Yes No**

2. How much is shown below? (*Write your answer on the line.*)

 = _____ cents

DAILY
Warm-Up 35

Name _____ Date _____

1. Which group has **fewer than 6** tools? (*Circle the correct letter.*)

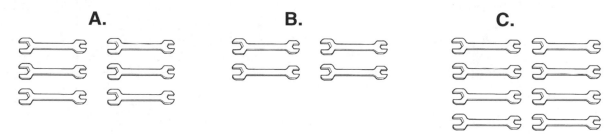

| A. | B. | C. |

2. What number is **greater than 14**? (*Circle the correct letter.*)

A. 13   **B.** 14   **C.** 15

DAILY
Warm-Up 36

Name _____ Date _____

1. What answer makes the number sentence **true**? (*Circle the correct letter.*)

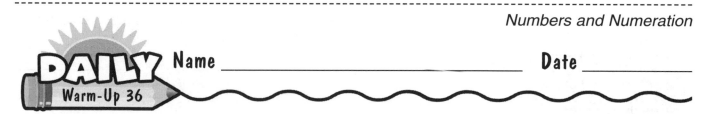

16 ◯ 18

A. >   **B.** <   **C.** =

2. Circle the **eighth** triangle.

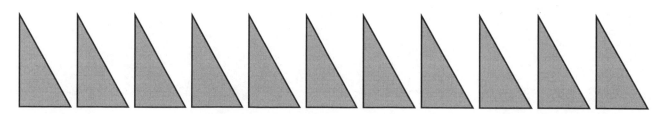

Jumping Up Learning Circles
5965 Almaden Expy Suite 165
San Jose, CA95120
408-323-8388

DAILY
Warm-Up 37

Name _____   Date _____

1. Look at the hundreds chart to solve the problem below.

1	2	3	4	5	6	7	8	9	10
11	12	13	14	15	16	17	18	19	20
21	22	23	24	25	26	27	28	29	30
31	32	33	34	35	36	37	38	39	40
41	42	43	44	45	46	47	48	49	50
51	52	53	54	55	56	57	58	59	60
61	62	63	64	65	66	67	68	69	70
71	72	73	74	75	76	77	78	79	80
81	82	83	84	85	86	87	88	89	90
91	92	93	94	95	96	97	98	99	100

• I am not an even number.

• I am larger than 20 but less than 40.

• My digits add up to 10.

What number am I? _____

2. Find the number of tens and ones, and then write the number.

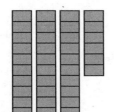

_____ tens and
_____ ones

Number: _____

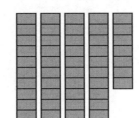

_____ tens and
_____ ones

Number: _____

DAILY
Warm-Up 38

Name _____   Date _____

1. Order the numbers from **largest to smallest**.

12   9   15

_____   _____   _____

2. Jack has 6 cubes. Jeff has 9 cubes. Jim has 4 cubes. Write the cubes each boy has from **smallest to largest**.

_____   _____   _____

DAILY
Warm-Up 39

Name _____ Date _____

1. Use the key to make the number sentences true.
Use every number from the box.

Key
33
18
65
40

35 > _____   _____ < 68

23 > _____   _____ < 43

2. Look at the shapes. What shape is **ninth** in line? (*Circle the correct letter.*)

square   heart   circle   circle   triangle   square   square   heart   circle

A. square   **B.** circle   **C.** heart   **D.** triangle

Numbers and Numeration

DAILY
Warm-Up 40

Name _____ Date _____

1. Count each group of shapes, and then write the number. Use the < (less
than), > (greater than), or = (equal to) symbol to compare the shapes.

  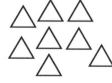 

_____ ◯ _____   _____ ◯ _____

2. Find the value of the coins below.

_____ cents   _____ cents

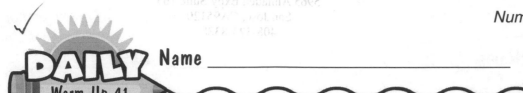

Name _____ **Date** _____

1. Circle **true** or **false**.

This coin is called a penny. **True** **False**

_____

This coin has a value of 5¢. **True** **False**

2. Which number has a 5 in the tens place and a 4 in the ones place? (*Circle the correct letter.*)

A. 52   **B.** 45   **C.** 51   **D.** 54

Name _____ **Date** _____

1. Which symbol belongs in the circle? (*Circle the correct letter.*)

12 ◯ 9

A. >   **B.** <   **C.** =

2. How many cubes are there in all?

There are _____ cubes.

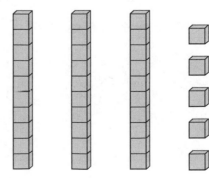

Name _____ **Date** _____

1. Answer the problems below.

What is the largest number you can make with the numbers on the T-shirts?

_____

What is the smallest number you can make with the numbers on the T-shirts?

_____

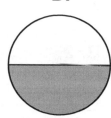

2. Circle the letter of the shape that matches $\frac{1}{4}$.

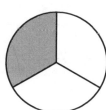 A.   B.   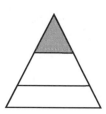 C.   D.

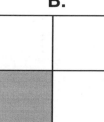

Name _____ **Date** _____

1. In the number **98**, which digit is in the **tens place**? *(Write the answer on the line.)*

_____

2. Circle the number that is **closest to 78**.

68   86   82

DAILY **Name** _____ **Date** _____
Warm-Up 45

1. How many of the faces out of the total are smiling? (*Circle the correct letter.*)

A. $\frac{2}{4}$ **B.** $\frac{2}{3}$ **C.** $\frac{4}{4}$ **D.** $\frac{2}{3}$

2. What number is missing on the number line? (*Circle the correct letter.*)

A. 25

B. 26

C. 27

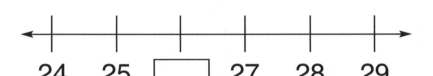

24   25   ☐   27   28   29

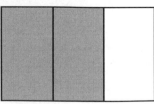

DAILY **Name** _____ **Date** _____
Warm-Up 46

1. Sam has **forty-three** baseball cards. How is the number read? (*Circle the correct letter.*)

A. 34   **B.** 43   **C.** 403

2. Which rectangle shows $\frac{2}{4}$ shaded? (*Circle the correct letter.*)

A.   **B.**   **C.**

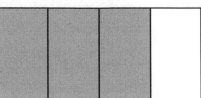 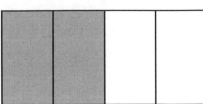

DAILY Warm-Up 47

Name _____ Date _____

1. Which calculator reads **9 tens + 6 ones**? (*Circle the correct letter.*)

A.	B.	C.	D.

2. Shade 46 on the hundreds chart below. (*Use your pencil.*)

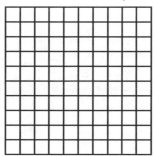

DAILY Warm-Up 48

Name _____ Date _____

1. Write the number below in words.

Tens	Ones
3	4

_____

2. Arrange these numbers to make the largest possible number. (*Write your answer on the line.*)

_____

| 0 | 2 | 1 |

Name _____ Date _____

DAILY Warm-Up 49

1. Solve the problem.

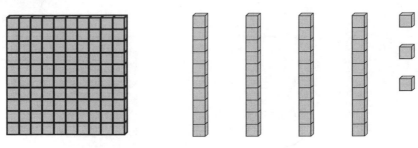

_____ hundred and _____ tens and _____ ones = _____

2. Fill in with the correct symbol (<, =, or >).

102 ◯ 104

Name _____ Date _____

DAILY Warm-Up 50

1. What numbers come **before and after** each number?

_____, 45, _____	_____, 26, _____	_____, 33, _____
_____, 27, _____	_____, 54, _____	_____, 20, _____
_____, 35, _____	_____, 67, _____	_____, 56, _____
_____, 40, _____	_____, 43, _____	_____, 87, _____

2. Fill in the correct symbol (<, =, or >).

16 ◯ 26

DAILY
Warm-Up 51

Name _____ Date _____

1. Name the fractions below.

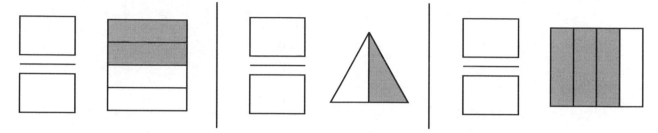

2. Which answer choice below is **false**? (*Circle the correct letter.*)

A. 50 > thirty-two

C. 24 > eighteen

B. 43 < forty-seven

D. 33 > thirty-seven

DAILY
Warm-Up 52

Name _____ Date _____

1. Which answer choice below is **true**? (*Circle the correct letter.*)

A. 19 = twenty-nine

C. 10 = twelve

B. 43 = forty-three

D. 87 = seventy-eight

2. How many cubes are below? (*Write the number in the chart.*)

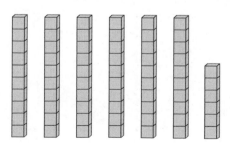

Tens	Ones

DAILY Name _____ **Date** _____

Warm-Up 53

1. Write the missing numbers.

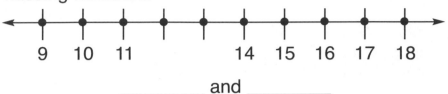

9   10   11   14   15   16   17   18

_____ and _____

2. How many paintbrushes does Mrs. Watkins have in her classroom?

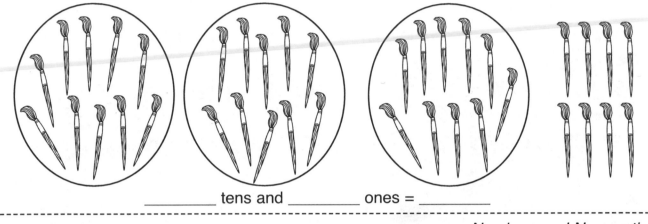

_____ tens and _____ ones = _____

DAILY Name _____ **Date** _____

Warm-Up 54

1. Mary has 87 stuffed animals. How do we write the number of Mary's stuffed animals? *(Circle the correct letter.)*

A. eighty-six   **B.** eighty-four   **C.** eighty-seven

2. What fraction of the shape is shaded? (*Write your answer on the line.*)

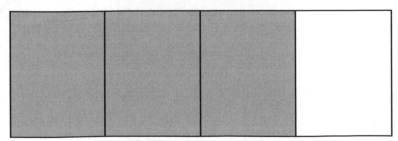

_____

DAILY Warm-Up 55   **Name** _____ **Date** _____

1. Round these numbers to the nearest 10.

Circle the number 23 falls closest to on the number line.

23   20   30   23 rounds to _____

Circle the number 36 falls closest to on the number line.

36   30   40   36 rounds to _____

2. Which answer choice below is **false**?

A. 98 > ninety-six   **B.** 73 < sixty-three   **C.** 54 > forty-two

---

DAILY Warm-Up 56   **Name** _____ **Date** _____

1. Which answer choice below is **true**?

A. 132 = one hundred forty-two

B. 87 = ninety-three

C. 115 = one hundred fifteen

2. Michael has 8 stacks of baseball cards. Each stack has 10 baseball cards. How many baseball cards does Michael have in all? (*Write your answer on the chart.*)

Tens	Ones

DAILY Warm-Up 57   Name _____   Date _____

1. Circle the fraction that names the shaded part.

$\dfrac{4}{3}$ $\dfrac{3}{4}$ $\dfrac{1}{2}$

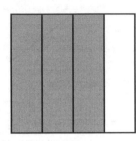

2. How much money do the coins show?

      + _____ = _____ cents

DAILY Warm-Up 58   Name _____   Date _____

1. Cindy found some money. How much money did Cindy find?

_____ ¢

2. Mary found 86 shells on the beach. Write the number of shells Mary found in word form.

_____

DAILY Warm-Up 59   Name _____   Date _____

1. Which group has more than 12 blocks? (*Circle the correct letter.*)

A.

B.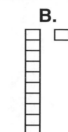

C.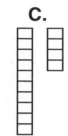

2. How many pieces of candy are in each group? Write the numbers on the lines below.

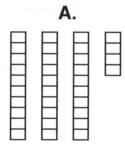 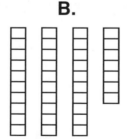 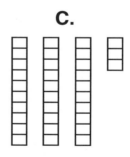

_____   _____   _____
- - - - - - - - - - -   - - - - - - - - - - -   - - - - - - - - - - -
_____   _____   _____

DAILY Warm-Up 60   Name _____   Date _____

1. Circle the letter of the group that is greater than 34.

A.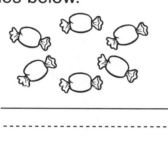

B.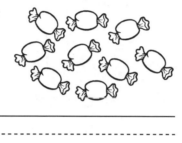

C.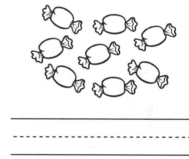

2. Which group of tally marks shows the number 19? (*Circle the correct letter.*)

A.

B.

C.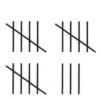

Name _____ **Date** _____

Warm-Up 61

1. How many tens and ones are shown below? (*Write your answer on the chart.*)

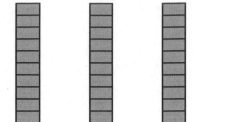 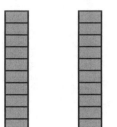

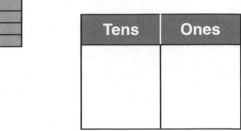

Tens	Ones

2. How many total balloons are there?

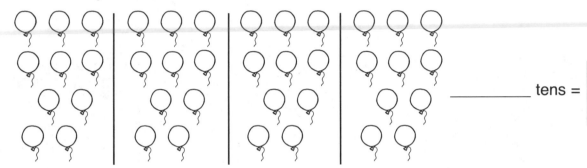

_____ tens =

- -

Name _____ **Date** _____

Warm-Up 62

1. Gene has 50¢ in his piggybank. He finds 10¢ and places it in the piggybank. How much money does Gene now have in his piggybank?

_____ ¢

2. Mark has 10¢. He spent 5¢ buying a piece of gum. How much money does Mark have left?

_____ ¢

Answer Key

Warm-Up 1
1. D
2.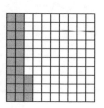

Warm-Up 2
1. eighteen   2. 65

Warm-Up 3
1. 10   2. D

Warm-Up 4
1. B   2. 4

Warm-Up 5
1. 43   2. 94

Warm-Up 6
1. A. 12
   B. 27
   C. 63
   D. 22
2. 2, 4, 6, and 8

Warm-Up 7
1.
2.

Warm-Up 8
1. C—twelve   2. 10, 8, 9

Warm-Up 9
1. $3 + 5 = 8$
2. 8, 5, 4, 9

Warm-Up 10
1.

	Tens	Ones
14 =	1	4
12 =	1	2
33 =	3	3

2. 4 tens 2 ones, 42
   5 tens 5 ones, 55
   2 tens 3 ones, 23

Warm-Up 11
1. C
2.

1	2	3	4	5	6	7	8	9	10
11	12	13	14	15	16	17	18	19	20
21	22	23	24	25	26	27	28	29	30
31	32	33	34	35	36	37	38	39	40
41	42	43	44	45	46	47	48	49	50
51	52	53	54	55	56	57	58	59	60
61	62	63	64	65	66	67	68	69	70
71	72	73	74	75	76	77	78	79	80
81	82	83	84	85	86	87	88	89	90
91	92	93	94	95	96	97	98	99	100

Warm-Up 12
1. C
2. Sample Answer:

Warm-Up 13
1. B
2. A—18
   B—35
   C—17
   D—27

Warm-Up 14
1. 27   2. C

Warm-Up 15
1. 17 and 18
2. 4 tens and 5 ones = 45

Warm-Up 16
1. 1 ten and 4 ones = 14
2. A. 1/2
   B. 2/3

Warm-Up 17
1.

5	10	15	20	25	30	35
40	45	50	55	60	65	70
75	80	85	90	95	100	105

2. 18

Warm-Up 18
1. A
2. 15, 14, 13, 11, 9, 7

Warm-Up 19
1. B
2. 16 > 12
   24 > 14
   31 > 13
   28 > 18

Warm-Up 20
1.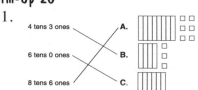
2. nine
   eight
   five

Warm-Up 21
1. No   2. 0, 2, 4, 6, 8

Warm-Up 22
1. Sample Answer:

2. No

Warm-Up 23
1. 60 cents
2. 4, 8, 12, 16

Warm-Up 24
1.
2. 45—forty-five

Warm-Up 25
1. C—seven
2. Sample Answer:

Warm-Up 26
1. A   2. C

Warm-Up 27
1. 4 cents
2. seven
   nine
   six

Warm-Up 28
1. 5, 7, 9, 11   2. B

Warm-Up 29
1. Sample Answer:

Answer Key

2.

Number: 5   Word: five

Warm-Up 30
1.

| 9 | 10 | 5 |

2. B

Warm-Up 31
1. A   2. C

Warm-Up 32
1. Sample
Answer:
2. B

Warm-Up 33
1. C
2.

Warm-Up 34
1. Yes, No, Yes
2. 10 cents

Warm-Up 35
1. B
2. C

Warm-Up 36
1. B
2.

Warm-Up 37
1. 37
2. 3 tens and 6 ones, 36
   4 tens and 7 ones, 47

Warm-Up 38
1. 15, 12, 9
2. 4, 6, 9

Warm-Up 39
1. 35 > 33
   23 > 18
   65 < 68
   40 < 43
2. B

Warm-Up 40
1. 6 > 3
   8 > 4
2. 12 cents
   7 cents

Warm-Up 41
1. True
   False
2. D

Warm-Up 42
1. A
2. 35

Warm-Up 43
1. 210
   102
2. D

Warm-Up 44
1. 9
2. 82

Warm-Up 45
1. A
2. B

Warm-Up 46
1. B
2. C

Warm-Up 47
1. C
2.

Warm-Up 48
1. thirty-four
2. 210

Warm-Up 49
1. 1 hundred and 4 tens and
   3 ones = 143
2. 102 < 104

Warm-Up 50
1. 44, 45, 46
   26, 27, 28
   34, 35, 36

39, 40, 41
25, 26, 27
53, 54, 55
66, 67, 68
42, 43, 44
32, 33, 34
19, 20, 21
55, 56, 57
86, 87, 88
2. 16 < 26

Warm-Up 51
1. 2/4, 1/2, 3/4
2. D

Warm-Up 52
1. B
2. 6 tens, 6 ones

Warm-Up 53
1. 12 and 13
2. 3 tens and 8 ones = 38

Warm-Up 54
1. C   2. 3/4

Warm-Up 55
1. 20
   40
2. B

Warm-Up 56
1. C
2. 8 tens, 0 ones

Warm-Up 57
1. 3/4   2. 48 cents

Warm-Up 58
1. 53¢
2. eighty-six

Warm-Up 59
1. C   2. 6, 9, 8

Warm-Up 60
1. B   2. A

Warm-Up 61
1. 5 tens, 4 ones
2. 4 tens = 40

Warm-Up 62
1. 60¢   2. 5¢

OPERATIONS

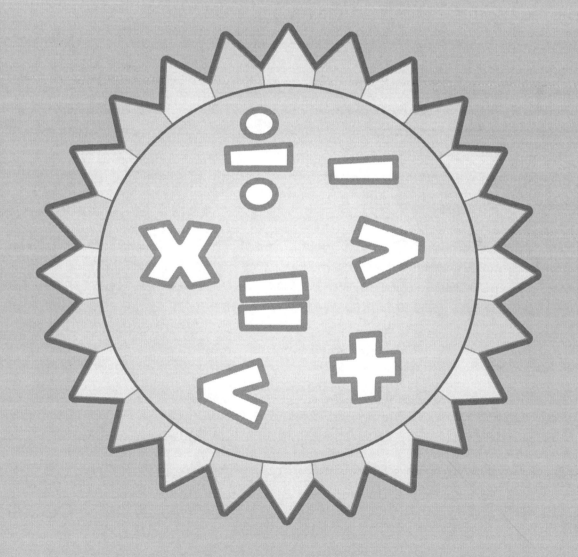

Name _____ **Date** _____

1. Sandra added 8 to a number and got the number shown on the calculator. What number did she add to make 12? *(Write your answer on the line.)*

_____

2. Tommy has 2 orange cubes and 3 yellow cubes. Mark has 4 orange cubes. How many orange cubes do Tommy and Mark have together?

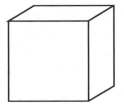

_____ orange cubes

Name _____ **Date** _____

1. Mary has 6 cookies. She gave 2 cookies to her sister. How many cookies does Mary have left? *(Circle the correct letter.)*

A.   **B.**   **C.**   **D.**

2. Write the answer to the problem below in the box.

$$5 - \boxed{} = 3$$

DAILY Warm-Up 3

Name _____ Date _____

1. Solve the problems below.

3	4	4	8
+ 4	+ 5	− 3	− 3

2. Mary has 2 cubes, 3 triangles, and 6 rectangles. How many total shapes does Mary have?

_____ shapes

 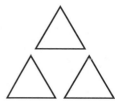 

- -

DAILY Warm-Up 4

Name _____ Date _____

1. Gene has 2 nickels, 3 pennies, and 4 dimes. How many coins does Gene have?

_____ coins

2. Sam scored 8 points playing basketball. Jennie scored 4 more points than Sam. How many points did Jennie score?

_____ points

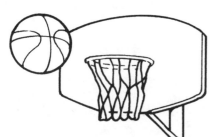

DAILY Warm-Up 5   Name _____   Date _____

1. How many total staplers does the problem show?

2. Solve the problem below.

$$14 + 8 = \boxed{}$$

DAILY Warm-Up 6   Name _____   Date _____

1. Diana invited 16 friends to her birthday party. Six friends did not come to the party. How many friends came to Diana's birthday party?

_____ friends

2. Pete bought 3 pair of socks. There are 2 socks in a pair. How many total socks did Pete buy?

DAILY Warm-Up 7   Name _____   Date _____

1. Use the numbers in the box to make a subtraction problem.

| 16 | 7 | 23 |

_____ – _____ = _____

2. How many total buttons are on all three dresses?

_____ buttons

DAILY Warm-Up 8   Name _____   Date _____

1. List sets of three numbers that add to 10. (*The first is done for you.*)

| 1 | + | 7 | + | 2 | = | 10 |

_____ + ⬭ + △ = 10

_____ + ⬭ + △ = 10

2. There are 5 cars in a parking lot. There are 2 trucks in the same parking lot. Then, 4 more cars park in the parking lot. How many cars are now parked in the parking lot?

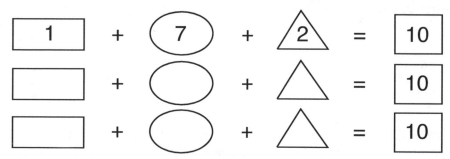

_____ cars

Name _____ **Date** _____

1. Yolanda picked seven roses yesterday. Today, Yolanda picked twelve roses. How many more roses did Yolanda pick today?

_____ roses

2. Write story problem for the number sentence below.

$$4 - 2 = ?$$

_____

_____

_____

Name _____ **Date** _____

1. At a beach, Jim found 6 large shells and 4 small shells. How many shells did he find in all?

_____ shells

2. Look at the shape equation. Which answer shows the number sentence that matches? (*Circle the correct letter.*)

A. 8 + 2 = 10   **C.** 6 − 2 = 4

B. 6 + 2 = 8   **D.** 4 − 2 = 2

Name _____ **Date** _____

Warm-Up 11

1. Joe bought a package of socks. There were 2 green socks, 2 red socks, and 2 white socks in the package. How many total socks were in the package?

_____ socks

2. Circle the correct answers.

3 + 3 = 9	**True**	**False**	2 + 4 = 7	**True**	**False**
9 − 3 = 6	**True**	**False**	7 − 5 = 2	**True**	**False**
5 + 2 = 8	**True**	**False**	4 + 2 = 6	**True**	**False**
6 − 3 = 4	**True**	**False**	8 − 3 = 5	**True**	**False**

Name _____ **Date** _____

Warm-Up 12

1. At the beach, you found 4 small shells and 9 large shells. How many shells did you find in all?

_____ shells

2. Write the answer to the problem below.

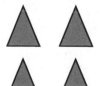 +  =

DAILY Warm-Up 13

Name _____ Date _____

1. Pete picked 8 apples from an apple tree. Jason picked 4 more than Pete. How many apples did Jason pick?

_____ apples

2. Fill in the correct symbol. Use the symbols <, >, or =.

13 ◯ 23

DAILY Warm-Up 14

Name _____ Date _____

1. Look at the scoreboard. How many more points did Luke score than Jim?

_____ more points

Score Board	
Jim	Luke
ꕯꕯꕯꕯꕯ ꕯꕯꕯ	ꕯꕯꕯꕯꕯ ꕯꕯꕯꕯꕯ ꕯꕯ

2. Solve the problem. Write the number.

 −  =

_____

Name _____   **Date** _____

Warm-Up 15

1. How many total apples are in all four baskets?

9 + 9 + 9 =   _____

2. Fred has 3 basketballs in each bag. He has 3 bags. How many basketballs does Fred have in all?

+   +   =   _____

Name _____   **Date** _____

Warm-Up 16

1. Fred has 8 tennis balls. He gave 3 tennis balls to his friend. How many tennis balls does Fred have left?

_____ tennis balls

2. Twelve people climbed a rope ladder to a tree house. 5 people climbed back down. How many people were still in the tree house?

_____ people

DAILY Warm-Up 17

Name _____   **Date** _____

1. Sammy has 4 apples and 6 oranges. Sue has 7 apples. How many apples do Sammy and Sue have in all?

_____ apples

2. Each pail of sand makes 1 castle. How many castles will 4 pails of sand make?

_____ castles

- -

DAILY Warm-Up 18

Name _____   **Date** _____

1. Find the answer to each problem. *(Circle the correct letter.)*

$15 - 8 =$
A. 9
B. 8
C. 7

$23 - 7 =$
A. 16
B. 17
C. 28

$19 - 7 =$
A. 11
B. 12
C. 13

2. Jim hit 3 home runs. Mike hit 4 more home runs than Jim. How many home runs did Mike hit?

Mike hit _____ home runs.

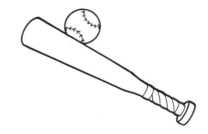

DAILY Warm-Up 19

Name _____ Date _____

1. Two students want to share 8 apples. How many apples will each student get?

Each student will get _____ apples.

2. Mike has 8 letters. He has 2 stamps. How many letters will not have a stamp?

_____ letters

DAILY Warm-Up 20

Name _____ Date _____

1. Matt brought 22 cupcakes to school. Nine cupcakes were eaten. How many cupcakes were left?

_____ cupcakes

2. Jake has 6 locks. He has 2 keys. How many locks to not have a key?

_____ locks

Name _____ **Date** _____

Warm-Up 21

1. Is the subtraction problem correct? *(Circle "Yes" or "No.")*

Yes   **No**

$$\begin{array}{r} 6 \\ -\ 5 \\ \hline 11 \end{array}$$

2. George has 6 nickels and 10 pennies. How many more pennies than nickels does George have?

_____ pennies

Name _____ **Date** _____

Warm-Up 22

1. How many more rectangles than circles are there?

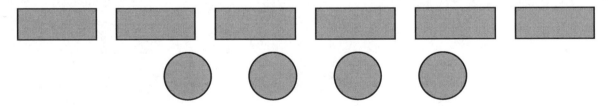

There are _____ more rectangles than circles.

2. You have 8 smiley-face stickers. You have 2 star stickers. How many more smiley-face stickers than star stickers do you have?

_____ more smiley-face stickers

Name _____ Date _____

DAILY Warm-Up 23

1. Fill in the boxes with your own numbers. Then subtract.

2. Circle groups of 5.

1   2   3   4   5   6   7   8   9   10

There are _____ groups of 5 in 10.

- -

DAILY Warm-Up 24

Name _____ Date _____

1. Circle groups of 2.

1   2   3   4   5   6   7   8   9   10

There are _____ groups of 2 in 10.

2. Circle groups of 4.

1   2   3   4   5   6   7   8

There are _____ groups of 4 in 8.

Name _____ **Date** _____

DAILY Warm-Up 25

1. Mandy has 10 blue ribbons for swimming. Peggy has 5 blue ribbons for swimming. How many more blue ribbons does Mandy have?

_____ blue ribbons

2. Solve the problems below.

$2 \times 4 =$ ☐

$4 + 4 =$ ☐

😊 😊 😊 😊 + 😊 😊 😊 😊 = _____

Name _____ **Date** _____

DAILY Warm-Up 26

1. There are 6 horses and 4 cows in a field. How many animals are in the field?

_____ animals

2. Michael has 5 green cubes, 3 yellow cubes, and 2 red cubes in a box. How many cubes are in the box?

_____ cubes

DAILY Warm-Up 27 **Name** _____ **Date** _____

1. There are 6 pencils in a package. How many pencils are in 2 packages?

There are _____ pencils in 2 packages.

2. There are 12 eggs in a dozen. How many eggs are in 2 dozen?

There are _____ eggs in 2 dozen.

DAILY Warm-Up 28 **Name** _____ **Date** _____

1. Sandra and Beth each picked 4 roses. How many roses did they pick altogether?

Sandra and Beth picked _____ roses altogether.

2. Jim bought 2 new fishing lures. Each fishing lure cost $5. How much did Jim spend?

Jim spent _____ .

Name _____ **Date** _____

1. Find the answer, and then write the number in the last circle.

2. Which answer is the same as 2 + 3 = ☐ ? *(Circle the correct letter.)*

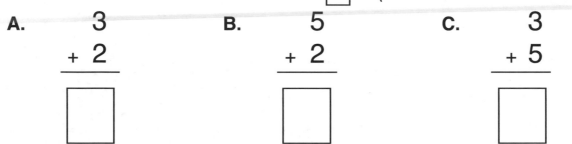

A.   3
     + 2
     ☐

B.   5
     + 2
     ☐

C.   3
     + 5
     ☐

- -

Name _____ **Date** _____

1. Look at the pictures below. Which number sentence matches the pictures? (*Circle the correct letter.*)

A. 4 − 1 =   **B.** 3 + 3 =   **C.** 3 + 4 =

2. Six 🚗 are parked in a parking lot. Then 3 more 🚗 park in the parking lot. How many 🚗 are now in the parking lot?

There are _____ 🚗 in the parking lot.

Name _____ **Date** _____

1. Your cat had 5 kittens. Three were black and the rest were white. How many kittens were white?

There were _____ white kittens.

2. I am 3 more than 5. What number am I? (*Circle the correct letter.*)

A. 2   **B.** 3   **C.** 8

- -

Name _____ **Date** _____

1. To find 3 fewer than 9, you should _____. (*Circle the correct letter.*)

A. add   **B.** subtract

2. Write the number in the circle. Then, circle the correct letter.

A. 1

B. 4

C. 5

 +  =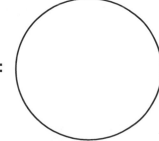

Operations

DAILY Warm-Up 33

Name _____ Date _____

1. Which problem equals 8? *(Circle the correct letter.)*

A.   7
   + 2
   [ ]

B.   5
   + 2
   [ ]

C.   6
   + 2
   [ ]

2. Find the missing numbers for the problems below.

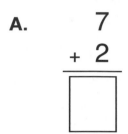

3
+ [ ]
[ ]

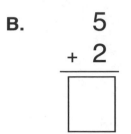

5
+ [ ]
8

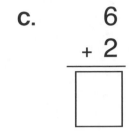

[ ]
+ 4
[ ]

Operations

DAILY Warm-Up 34

Name _____ Date _____

1. Circle the picture that shows 2 + 5.

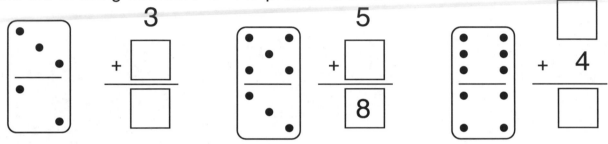

2. Hank has 6 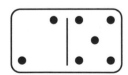. He gives 2 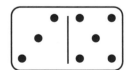 to his neighbor. How many 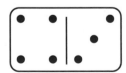 does Hank have left?

Hank has _____  left.

#3959 Daily Warm-Ups: Math   58   ©Teacher Created Resources, Inc.

Name _____ **Date** _____

1. There are 4 🐕 in the yard and 2 🐕 in the house. How many dogs are there in all?

There are _____ 🐕 altogether.

2. Find the answer, and then write the number in the last circle.

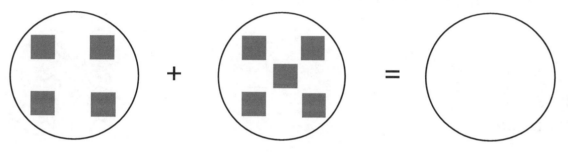

Name _____ **Date** _____

1. Jim opened 4 🎁 from his parents and 2 🎁 from his grandparents. How many presents did he open in all?

Jim opened _____ 🎁 in all.

2. Which answer is the same as 6 + 3 = ☐ ? *(Circle the correct letter.)*

A. $\begin{array}{r} 9 \\ + 2 \\ \hline \ \end{array}$ **B.** $\begin{array}{r} 6 \\ + 2 \\ \hline \ \end{array}$ **C.** $\begin{array}{r} 6 \\ + 3 \\ \hline \ \end{array}$

Name _____ Date _____

1. What is 8 – 3? (*Circle the correct letter.*)

A. 11   **B.** 6   **C.** 5

2. Mary has 5 dolls. Cindy has some dolls. Together Mary and Cindy have 9 dolls. How many dolls does Cindy have?

Cindy has _____ dolls.

DAILY Warm-Up 38

Name _____ Date _____

1. Jackie has 6 cubes in a bag. Three of the cubes are blue. The rest of the cubes are orange. How many cubes are orange?

_____ cubes are orange.

2. Margo has 5 ✏ and 2 pairs of ✄ . Linda has 4 ✏ . How many ✏ do Margo and Linda have in all?

They have _____ ✏ in all.

DAILY Name _____ Date _____
Warm-Up 39

1. Mark has 8 coins. Three coins are nickels and the rest are pennies. How many coins are pennies? (*Circle the correct letter.*)

A. 6   **B.** 5   **C.** 4

2. What number sentence does the picture below show? (*Circle the correct letter.*)

A. 6 + 2 = 8   **B.** 6 − 2 = 4   **C.** 6 − 3 = 3

DAILY Name _____ Date _____
Warm-Up 40

1. Michael saw 9 🕊 flying in the sky. Two 🕊 landed. How many 🕊 are still flying in the sky?

There are _____ 🕊 flying in the sky.

2. Look at the number line. If the ball rolls back 3 numbers, where will it land?

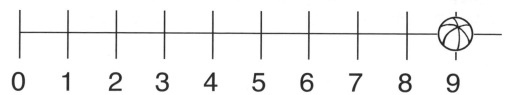

The 🏀 will land on the number _____ .

Name _____ **Date** _____

1. Which number sentence shows the cube being moved 3 spaces forward?

   0   1   2   3   4   5   6   7   8   9

A. $2 + 5 = 7$ **B.** $2 + 3 = 5$ **C.** $3 + 5 = 8$

2. Nine 🧍 came into the store. Then, 3 🧍 left. How many 🧍 were left in the store?

There were _____ 🧍 left in the store.

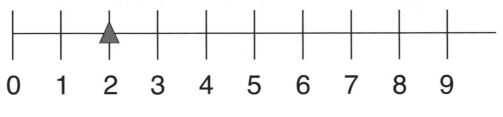

Name _____ **Date** _____

1. Look at the triangle. Move it 5 spaces forward. Where is it now?

   0   1   2   3   4   5   6   7   8   9

A. 7   **B.** 6   **C.** 5

2. Mary bought 2 packages of gum. Each package had 4 sticks of gum. How many sticks of gum are there in all? (*Solve by drawing a picture or using numbers.*)

_____ sticks of gum

Name _____ **Date** _____

Warm-Up 43

1. Which number sentence makes 12? (*Circle the correct letter.*)

   A. 6 + 5 =   **B.** 7 + 5 =   **C.** 8 + 5 =

2. Sandra has 5 orange buttons and 4 yellow buttons. Yolanda has 6 orange buttons. How many orange buttons do Sandra and Yolanda have in all? (*Circle the correct letter.*)

   A. 9

   B. 15

   C. 11

Name _____ **Date** _____

Warm-Up 44

1. There are 5 gray ducks and 4 white ducks swimming in a pond. How many ducks are there in all? (*Circle the correct letter and write your answer in the box.*)

   A. 5 − 4 = ☐   **B.** 5 + 4 = ☐   **C.** 5 + 5 = ☐

2. There are 12 chickens in a pen. Five chickens lay eggs. How many chickens do **NOT** lay eggs?

_____ chickens do not lay eggs.

DAILY
Warm-Up 45

Name _____ Date _____

1. Peggy has 5  . Mattie has 7 . What number sentence tells how many Peggy and Mattie have in all? (*Circle the correct letter.*)

A. 7 – 5 = 2   **B.** 7 + 5 = 11   **C.** 5 + 7 = 12

2. Two children plan to share 6 cookies. Circle to show how each child can get an equal share of the cookies.

DAILY
Warm-Up 46

Name _____ Date _____

1. James has 6 blue cubes, 6 orange cubes, and 6 green cubes. How many cubes does James have in all? (*Circle the correct letter.*)

A. 6   **B.** 12   **C.** 18

2. Three friends plan to share 9 pencils. Circle to show how each friend can get an equal number of pencils.

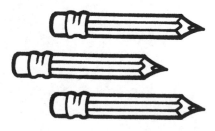
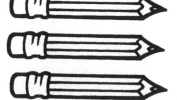

DAILY **Name** _____ **Date** _____
Warm-Up 47

1. Jennifer bought 12 books. During the summer, she read 5 books. How many books does she still need to read?

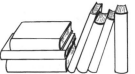

Jennifer needs to read _____ more books.

2. In a field, there are 14 white cows and 7 black cows. There are 4 horses in a pen. How many cows are there in all?

A. 18 **B.** 21 **C.** 25

DAILY **Name** _____ **Date** _____
Warm-Up 48

1. Margo brought 20 cookies to a party. Linda bought 10 cookies to the party. How many cookies did Margo and Linda bring in all? (*Show your work.*)

Margo and Linda brought _____ cookies in all.

2. Hannah has 16 stuffed animals on a shelf. She gave away 4 stuffed animals. How many stuffed animals does Hannah have left on the shelf? (*Circle the correct letter.*)

A. 20 **B.** 18 **C.** 12

DAILY Warm-Up 49

Name _____ Date _____

1. Linda found 22 large seashells and 43 small seashells on a beach. What should you do to find how many seashells Linda found in all? (*Circle the correct letter.*)

   A. subtract   **B.** add

2. Jimmy has 37 baseball cards in a large box. He has 22 baseball cards in a smaller box. Which sentence shows how many baseball cards Jimmy has in all? (*Circle the correct letter.*)

   A. Jimmy has 15 baseball cards in all.

   B. Jimmy has 60 baseball cards in all.

   C. Jimmy has 59 baseball cards in all.

DAILY Warm-Up 50

Name _____ Date _____

1. Sarah has 4 jars. There are 10 buttons in each jar. How many buttons does Sarah have in all? (*Show how you got your answer.*)

   Sarah has _____ buttons in all.

2. Pete bought a dozen doughnuts. Circle one dozen doughnuts.

Name _____ **Date** _____

Warm-Up 51

1. Six students planned to write 2 letters each to their favorite teacher. How many total letters did they write? (*Draw a picture.*)

They wrote _____ letters.

2. What is the difference between 3 and 14? (*Write your answer on the line.*)

_____

Name _____ **Date** _____

Warm-Up 52

1. Sammy found 3 pennies, 3 dimes, and 3 nickels on the playground. How much money did Sammy find?

A. 9¢   **B.** 48¢   **C.** 52¢

2. A dog has 4 legs. How many legs do 2 dogs have? (*Draw a picture.*)

They have _____ legs.

Name _____ **Date** _____

1. Which problem does **NOT** equal 14? (*Circle the correct letter.*)

A.   9
       + 5
      ☐

B.   8
       + 6
      ☐

C.   7
       + 8
      ☐

2. Find the missing addition facts for each problem.

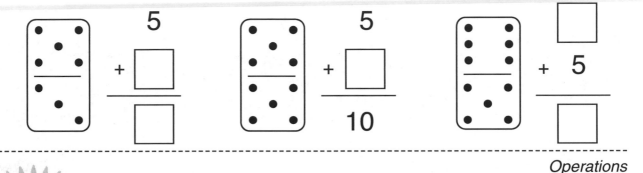

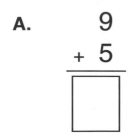

Name _____ **Date** _____

1. Circle the picture that shows 4 + 3 = 7.

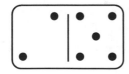   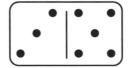   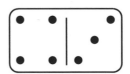

2. Five students played on the playground. Eight more students joined them. How many students played on the playground in all?

There were _____ students on the playground.

DAILY Name _____ Date _____

Warm-Up 55

1. Which number sentence makes 15? (*Circle the correct letter.*)

A. 7 + 7 =   **B.** 9 + 5 =   **C.** 8 + 7 =

2. If six students each need two sheets of paper, how many sheets of paper do they need in all? (*Circle the correct letter.*)

A. 6   **B.** 8   **C.** 12

DAILY Name _____ Date _____

Warm-Up 56

1. Mary has 6 sticks of gum. She gave 2 to Henry, 1 to Lynn, and 1 to Betty. How many sticks of gum does Mary have left?

Mary has _____ sticks of gum left.

2. Cindy has 9 coins in her piggybank. Three of them are pennies. The rest are dimes. How many coins are dimes?

There are _____ dimes in the piggybank.

DAILY Warm-Up 57   Name _____   Date _____

1. Jimmy bought 2 baseball cards for $1. How much money will 6 baseball cards cost? (*Draw a picture.*)

   A. $9

   B. $6

   C. $3

2. Mike had stamps for 3 of his 9 letters. How many stamps does he still need?

He still needs _____ stamps.

DAILY Warm-Up 58   Name _____   Date _____

1. Three orange shirts, 2 blue shirts, and 4 yellow shirts were bought for a student. How many shirts were bought for the student?

There were _____ shirts bought for the student.

2. Linda gave 3 pencils to Jake and 2 pencils to Cindy. Linda now has 4 pencils left. How many pencils did Linda have at the beginning?

Linda had _____ pencils at the beginning.

DAILY Warm-Up 59   Name _____   Date _____

1. Terry piled pennies in stacks of 10. She had 6 stacks. How many pennies did she have in all?

Terry has _____ pennies.

2. Tommy's cat had 6 kittens. Four were given away to friends. What should you do to find how many kittens were left? (*Circle the correct letter.*)

A. add   **B.** subtract

DAILY Warm-Up 60   Name _____   Date _____

1. Robin bought 18 cookies. She gave 4 to Maci and 3 to Ty. How many cookies does Robin have left? (*Circle the correct letter.*)

A. 25 cookies

B. 14 cookies

C. 11 cookies

2. Margaret gave three cookies to each of her six friends who came to her party. How many cookies did she give in all? (*Draw a picture.*)

Margaret gave _____ cookies in all.

DAILY Warm-Up 61

Name _____ **Date** _____

1. Mark swam 4 laps in the pool. Terry swam 2 more laps than Mark. Which number sentence shows the number of laps Terry swam? (*Circle the correct letter.*)

A. 4 − 2 = 2   **B.** 4 + 2 = 6   **C.** 6 + 2 = 8

2. Gordon rode 8 miles to school this morning. That afternoon, he rode back home. How many miles did he ride in all?

Gordon rode _____ miles.

DAILY Warm-Up 62

Name _____ **Date** _____

1. There are 15 basketballs in gym class. There are 8 students. If each student uses 1 basketball, how many basketballs are **NOT** being used?

_____ basketballs are not being used.

2. A box had 18 hair ribbons inside. Mary took out half the hair ribbons. How many hair ribbons were left?

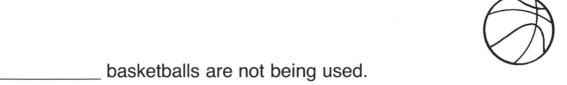

A. 18   **B.** 27   **C.** 9

Answer Key

Warm-Up 1
1. 4
2. 6

Warm-Up 2
1. D
2. 2

Warm-Up 3
1. 7, 9, 1, 5
2. 11

Warm-Up 4
1. 9
2. 12

Warm-Up 5
1. 11
2. 22

Warm-Up 6
1. 10
2. 6

Warm-Up 7
1. $23 - 16 = 7$ or $23 - 7 = 16$
2. 27 buttons

Warm-Up 8
1. Answers will vary.
2. 9

Warm-Up 9
1. 5
2. Answers will vary.

Warm-Up 10
1. 10
2. C

Warm-Up 11
1. 6
2. False   False
   True   True
   False   True
   False   True

Warm-Up 12
1. 13
2. 15

Warm-Up 13
1. 12
2. $13 < 23$

Warm-Up 14
1. 4
2. 5

Warm-Up 15
1. 27
2. 9

Warm-Up 16
1. 5
2. 7

Warm-Up 17
1. 11
2. 4

Warm-Up 18
1. C, A, B
2. 7

Warm-Up 19
1. 4
2. 6

Warm-Up 20
1. 13
2. 4

Warm-Up 21
1. No
2. 4

Warm-Up 22
1. 2
2. 6

Warm-Up 23
1. Answers will vary.
2. 2

Warm-Up 24
1. 5
2. 2

Warm-Up 25
1. 5
2. 8, 8, 8

Warm-Up 26
1. 10
2. 10

Warm-Up 27
1. 12
2. 24

Warm-Up 28
1. 8
2. $10

Warm-Up 29
1. 10
2. A

Warm-Up 30
1. C
2. 9

Warm-Up 31
1. 2
2. C

Warm-Up 32
1. B
2. 5, C

Warm-Up 33
1. C
2. $3 + \underline{2} = \underline{5}$
   $5 + \underline{3} = 8$
   $\underline{6} + 4 = \underline{10}$

Warm-Up 34
1.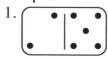
2. 4

Warm-Up 35
1. 6
2. 9

Warm-Up 36
1. 6
2. C

Warm-Up 37
1. C
2. 4

Answer Key

Warm-Up 38
1. 3
2. 9

Warm-Up 39
1. B
2. B

Warm-Up 40
1. 7
2. 6

Warm-Up 41
1. B
2. 6

Warm-Up 42
1. A
2. 8

Warm-Up 43
1. B
2. C

Warm-Up 44
1. B, 9
2. 7

Warm-Up 45
1. C
2. 3 cookies in each circle

Warm-Up 46
1. C
2. 3 pencils in each circle

Warm-Up 47
1. 7
2. B

Warm-Up 48
1. 20 + 10 = 30, 30
2. C

Warm-Up 49
1. B
2. C

Warm-Up 50
1. 10 + 10 + 10 + 10 = 40, 40
2. 12 doughnuts should be circled.

Warm-Up 51
1. 12
2. 11

Warm-Up 52
1. B
2. 8

Warm-Up 53
1. C
2. 5 + 3 = 8
   5 + 5 = 10
   6 + 5 = 11

Warm-Up 54
1. [domino image]
2. 13

Warm-Up 55
1. C
2. C

Warm-Up 56
1. 2
2. 6

Warm-Up 57
1. C
2. 6

Warm-Up 58
1. 9
2. 9

Warm-Up 59
1. 60
2. B

Warm-Up 60
1. C
2. 18

Warm-Up 61
1. B
2. 16

Warm-Up 62
1. 7
2. C

MEASUREMENT AND GEOMETRY

Name _____ **Date** _____

1. Which line is the **longest**? (*Circle the correct letter.*)

A. ▬▬▬▬▬▬▬▬▬

B. ▬▬▬▬▬▬▬▬▬▬▬

C. ▬▬▬▬▬

D. ▬▬▬▬▬▬▬▬▬▬▬▬

2. What time does the clock read? (*Circle the correct letter.*)

A. 12:00

B. 12:25

C. 5:00

D. 2:00

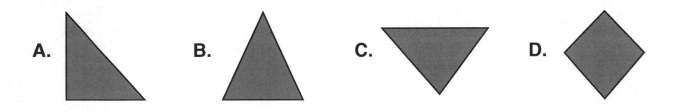

Name _____ **Date** _____

1. Which shape is **NOT** a triangle? (*Circle the correct letter.*)

A.   **B.**   **C.**   **D.**

2. Look at the shape. Are both sides the same? (*Circle your answer.*)

Yes   **No**

Name _____ **Date** _____

Warm-Up 3

1. **About** how many presents can fit along the line?

_____ presents

2. Look at the cups below. Which cup is the **tallest**? (*Circle the correct letter.*)

A.   **B.**   **C.**

Name _____ **Date** _____

Warm-Up 4

1. Margo left her house to go shopping at 10:00 A.M. She arrived home
   2 hours later. What time did she arrive home? (*Circle the correct letter.*)

   A. 8:00   **C.** 11:00

   B. 10:00   **D.** 12:00

2. Circle the container that will hold the **most** liquid.

DAILY Warm-Up 5

Name _____ Date _____

1. Which shape is the same size and shape as the shaded figure? (*Circle the correct letter.*)

         A.   **B.**   **C.**

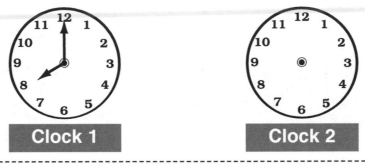

2. Look at the two clocks. Mark 10 minutes later on the second clock.

Clock 1   **Clock 2**

DAILY Warm-Up 6

Name _____ Date _____

1. Circle the rectangles below.

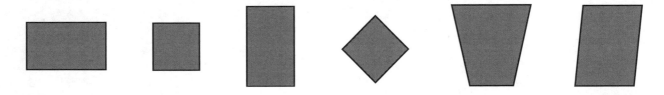

2. Read the time on the clocks. Show 10 minutes later on all four clocks.

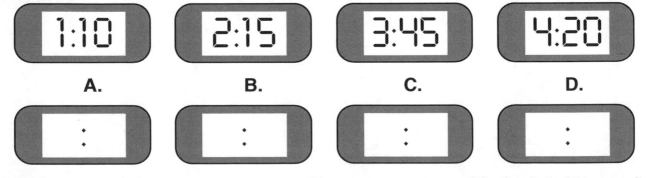

    A.   **B.**   **C.**   **D.**

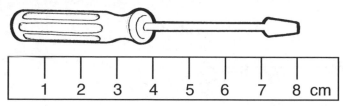

Name _____ Date _____

1. About how many centimeters long is the screwdriver?

```
1   2   3   4   5   6   7   8  cm
```

_____ centimeters

2. Write the clocks hands to show the time under each clock.

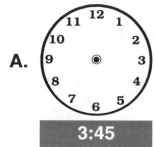 **A.**   **3:45**   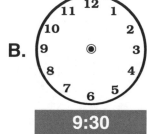 **B.**   **9:30**   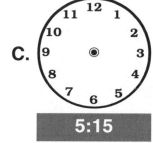 **C.**   **5:15**   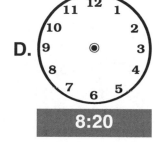 **D.**   **8:20**

- -

Name _____ Date _____

1. Name this figure. (*Circle the correct letter.*)

A. cube

B. rectangular prism

C. cylinder

D. sphere

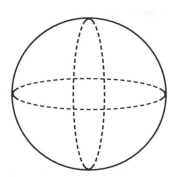

2. Draw a cone.

Name _____ **Date** _____

1. Use the pig counter to estimate the length of the marker.

The marker = _____ pig counters

2. What time comes after 3:10 P.M.? (*Circle the correct letter.*)

A. 12:05 P.M.   **C.** 3:00 P.M.

B. 2:30 P.M.   **D.** 3:30 P.M.

Name _____ **Date** _____

1. Which shape has the most sides? (*Circle the correct letter.*)

A.   **B.**   **C.**   **D.**

2. Match each solid shape with the correct letter.

cube   _____

rectangular prism _____

sphere   _____

cylinder   _____

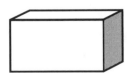

A.   **B.**

C.   **D.**

DAILY Warm-Up 11

Name _____ Date _____

1. About how many apples will fit inside the line?

_____ apples

2. Which clock below reads **10:00**? (*Circle the correct letter.*)

A. **B.** **C.** **D.**

DAILY Warm-Up 12

Name _____ Date _____

1. About how many paper clips long is the paintbrush?

This paintbrush is about _____ paper clips long.

2. About how many paper clips long is the pencil? (*Circle the correct letter.*)

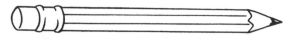

A. 2   **B.** 3   **C.** 4   **D.** 5

Name _____ **Date** _____

1. On this bowl, are both sides of the dashed line the same? (*Circle the correct answer.*)

Yes   **No**

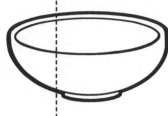

2. A movie started at 1:00. It ended 2 hours later. Show what time the movie ended.

Started

Ended

Name _____ **Date** _____

1. Circle the object that holds the **least** liquid.

2. Circle the object that holds the **most** liquid.

         ©*Teacher Created Resources, Inc.*

DAILY **Name** _____ **Date** _____
Warm-Up 15

1. How many pounds do the bricks weigh? (*Circle the correct letter.*)

A. 2 pounds

B. 3 pounds

C. 4 pounds

D. 5 pounds

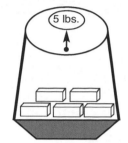

2. Circle the letter of the object that weighs the **least**.

 **A.**   **B.**    **C.**

DAILY **Name** _____ **Date** _____
Warm-Up 16

1. Circle the letter of the object that weighs the **least**.

A.    **B.**    **C.**

2. Are the two shapes the same? (*Circle your answer.*)

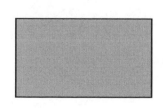

Yes

No

DAILY Warm-Up 17   Name _____   Date _____

1. Mark stacked two stacks of rectangular blocks. Which stack is **taller**? (*Circle the picture.*)

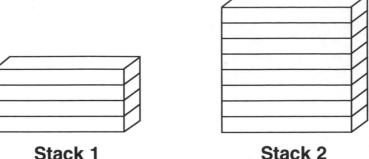

Stack 1   **Stack 2**

2. Which line is the **shortest**? (*Circle the correct letter.*)

A. ▬▬▬▬▬▬▬▬▬▬

B. ▬▬▬▬▬▬▬

C. ▬▬▬▬▬▬▬▬

DAILY Warm-Up 18   Name _____   Date _____

1. Gene put blocks on one side of a balance scale and books on the other side. Which side is **lighter**? (*Circle the correct letter.*)

A. blocks

B. books

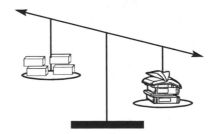

2. Circle the number that comes **before 8**.

0   1   2   3   4   5   6   7   8   9

Name _____ **Date** _____

1. Which can be used to measure length? (*Circle the correct letter.*)

A.  **B.** 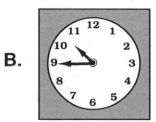 **C.**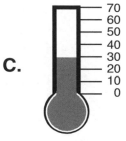

2. About how many insects long is the tool?

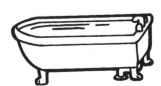

_____ insects

Name _____ **Date** _____

1. Circle the object that holds the **most** liquid.

2. How many centimeters long is the toothbrush?

_____ centimeters

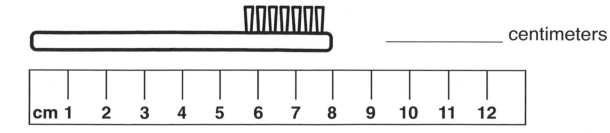

Name _____ **Date** _____

1. Which shape is a **circle**? (*Circle the correct letter.*)

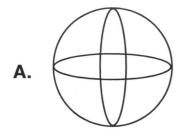 **A.**    **B.**   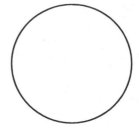 **C.**

2. Color the triangles blue.

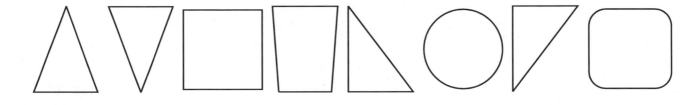

Name _____ **Date** _____

1. Look at the rectangle, and then answer the questions.

How many sides? _____

How many corners? _____

2. Look at the shapes. Color the rectangle blue. Color the triangle yellow.
Color the square red. Color the circle orange.

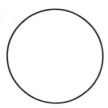   

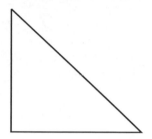

Name _____ **Date** _____

Warm-Up 23

1. Put an **X** on the shape that is **NOT** a triangle.

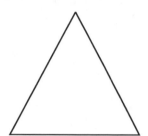
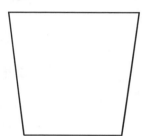
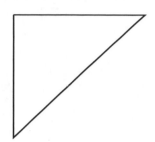

2. Which clock reads **5:15**? (*Circle the correct letter.*)

A.    **B.**    **C.**

Name _____ **Date** _____

Warm-Up 24

1. Circle the shape with the **most sides**.

2. How many **sides** does a square have? (*Circle the correct letter.*)

A. 2

B. 4

C. 6

Name _____ **Date** _____

Warm-Up 25

1. Which container holds the most? (*Circle the correct letter.*)

A. gallon   **B.** quart   **C.** pint

2. Write the time the clock shows.

   _____

Name _____ **Date** _____

Warm-Up 26

1. Circle the shape that does **NOT** belong.

2. Find the **area** of the shapes below.

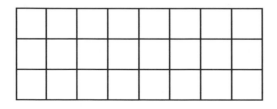   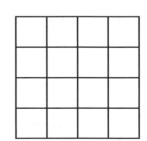

_____ square units   _____ square units

Name _____ **Date** _____

DAILY
Warm-Up 27

1. Which line is the longest? (*Circle the correct letter.*)

A.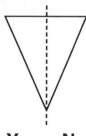

B.

C.

2. Look at the digital clock. Draw hands on the other clock showing what the time reads.

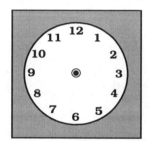

DAILY
Warm-Up 28

Name _____ **Date** _____

1. Look at the shapes. Are these the lines of symmetry? (*Circle "Yes" or "No."*)

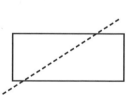

Yes   No   **Yes   No**   **Yes   No**   **Yes   No**

2. Is the shape below a circle? (*Circle "Yes" or "No."*)

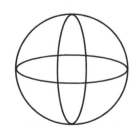

Yes

No

DAILY
Warm-Up 29

Name _____ Date _____

1. Which is the **heaviest**? (*Circle the correct letter.*)

A. 3 grams   **B.** 13 grams   **C.** 30 grams

2. Mark hands on the clock showing **2:25**.

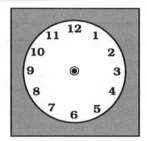

DAILY
Warm-Up 30

Name _____ Date _____

1. On what day of the week is March 25th?

_____

March						
SUNDAY	MONDAY	TUESDAY	WEDNESDAY	THURSDAY	FRIDAY	SATURDAY
		1	2	3	4	5
6	7	8	9	10	11	12
13	14	15	16	17	18	19
20	21	22	23	24	25	26
27	28	29	30	31		

2. Look at the shapes. Draw a line from the name to the correct shape.

triangle   **rectangle**   **circle**   **square**

Name _____   **Date** _____

1. Circle the **heaviest** object.

2. About how many paper clips long is the line?

The line is about _____ paper clips long.

Name _____   **Date** _____

1. Circle the **lightest** object.

 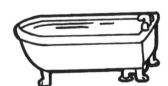 

2. Circle the rectangles.

Name _____ **Date** _____

DAILY Warm-Up 33

1. What day of the week is the 4th of August?

August 2005						
Sunday	Monday	Tuesday	Wednesday	Thursday	Friday	Saturday
	1	2	3	4	5	6

2. Circle the shape the does **NOT** belong with the others.

Name _____ **Date** _____

DAILY Warm-Up 34

1. Write how many **sides** are on each shape.

_____ sides   _____ sides

2. Draw a line on the shape showing two equal parts.

DAILY Warm-Up 35

Name _____ **Date** _____

1. Circle the time that is **longer**.

A. 10 hours   **B.** 10 days

2. Are the two shapes alike or different? *(Circle your answer.)*

Alike   **Different**

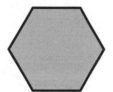

DAILY Warm-Up 36

Name _____ **Date** _____

1. Which shape does **NOT** belong? *(Circle the correct letter.)*

   A.   **B.**   **C.**

          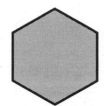

2. Circle the letter of the object in each group that holds more than 1 liter.

 = 1 liter

   A.   **B.** | **A.**   **B.**

          |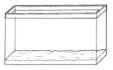

Name _____   **Date** _____

Warm-Up 37

1. Circle the letter that names the shape.

A. square

B. triangle

C. rectangle

2. Which clock shows **1:15**? (*Circle the correct letter.*)

A.   B.   C.

Name _____   **Date** _____

Warm-Up 38

1. Copy the closed shape.

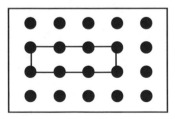   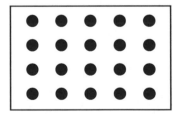

2. Is this shape a circle or a sphere?

The shape is a _____.

Name _____ **Date** _____

DAILY
Warm-Up 39

1. Estimate how many faces long the pencil is.

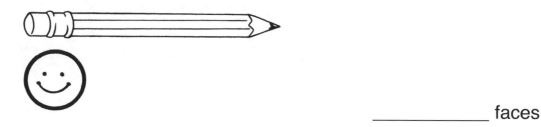

_____ faces

2. A rectangle has 4 corners and 5 sides. (*Circle your answer.*)

True   **False**

Name _____ **Date** _____

DAILY
Warm-Up 40

1. Draw a closed shape.

2. Draw a circle inside a rectangle.

Name _____ **Date** _____

Warm-Up 41

1. Are both sides the same? (*Circle your answers.*)

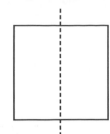 **Yes   No**   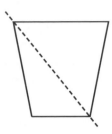 **Yes   No**

2. Which clock shows **10:10**? (*Circle the correct letter.*)

A.   **B.**   **C.**   **D.**

- -

Name _____ **Date** _____

Warm-Up 42

1. Describe how the two shapes are different.

   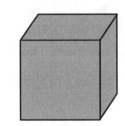   _____
                                      _____
                                      _____
                                      _____
                                      _____

2. Which shape is a **circle**?

A. 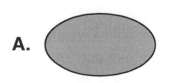   **B.** 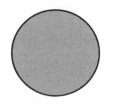   **C.** 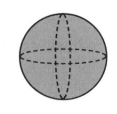   **D.**

DAILY
Warm-Up 43

Name _____ Date _____

1. Circle the letter of the shape that does **NOT** belong with the others.

A. 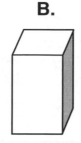 **B.** 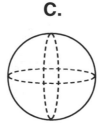 **C.** 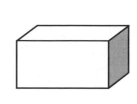 **D.**

2. Answer the questions below.

There are _____ minutes in an hour.

There are _____ seconds in a minute.

DAILY
Warm-Up 44

Name _____ Date _____

1. Circle the letter of the clock that shows **10:00**.

A.    **B.**

2. Circle the letter of the container that holds the **most** liquid.

A.    **B.**   **C.**

1. How many centimeters long is the paintbrush?

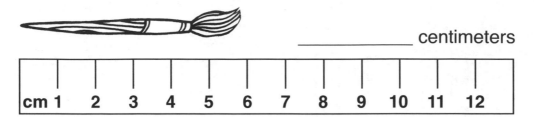

_____ centimeters

2. With your pencil, shade in all the flat shapes.

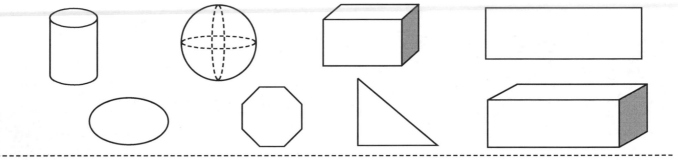

- -

1. Which object holds **more than a gallon**? (*Circle the correct letter.*)

A. spoon   **B.** bathtub

2. Look at the shapes on the bracelet. Color the spheres red.

DAILY
Warm-Up 47

1. About how many cubes long is the comb below?

_____ cubes

2. Use the calendar to answer the question.

How many days are in the month of May?

May						
SUNDAY	**MONDAY**	**TUESDAY**	**WEDNESDAY**	**THURSDAY**	**FRIDAY**	**SATURDAY**
1	2	3	4	5	6	7
8	9	10	11	12	13	14
15	16	17	18	19	20	21
22	23	24	25	26	27	28
29	30	31				

_____ days

DAILY
Warm-Up 48

1. How many grams does the bottle of glue weigh?
   (*Circle the correct letter.*)

   A. 12 grams

   B. 8 grams

   C. 6 grams

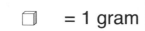 = 1 gram

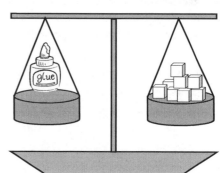

2. Circle the letter of the month that comes before May.

   A. June   **B.** July   **C.** April

Name _____ **Date** _____

1. How many sides does this shape have?

_____ sides

2. Use the key to name the shapes below.

Key	
A.	Sphere
B.	Circle
C.	Rectangle
D.	Triangle

_____ _____ _____ _____

Name _____ **Date** _____

1. Answer the questions below.

What is the name of the month?_____

How many days are in this month? _____

On what day of the week is the 31st?

_____

May						
SUNDAY	MONDAY	TUESDAY	WEDNESDAY	THURSDAY	FRIDAY	SATURDAY
1	2	3	4	5	6	7
8	9	10	11	12	13	14
15	16	17	18	19	20	21
22	23	24	25	26	27	28
29	30	31				

2. How many centimeters long is the pencil?

_____ centimeters

cm 1 2 3 4 5 6 7 8 9 10 11 12

DAILY Warm-Up 51

Name _____ Date _____

1. How far is each line in centimeters?

A. ━━━━━━━━━━━━━━━━ = _____ cm

B. ━━━━━━━━━━━━━━━━━━ = _____ cm

cm 1   2   3   4   5   6   7   8   9   10 11 12

2. Which shape does **NOT** belong with the others? *(Circle the correct letter.)*

     A.   **B.**   **C.**   **D.**

DAILY Warm-Up 52

Name _____ Date _____

1. Circle the rectangles.

2. How many days come between Sunday and Saturday?

There are _____ days between Sunday and Saturday.

DAILY
Warm-Up 53

Name _____ Date _____

1. Look at the clock. Write what the time was one hour before.

It was [:   ] .

2. Draw the clock hands to show **7:30**.

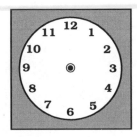

DAILY
Warm-Up 54

Name _____ Date _____

1. Circle **true** or **false**.

This shape is a cylinder.

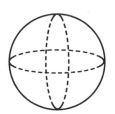

True   **False**

2. Look at each clock. Draw clock hands showing the correct time that is under each clock.

1:15

1:30

1:45

2:00

Name _____ **Date** _____

Warm-Up 55

1. Answer **true** or **false** for the problems below.

A washing machine holds more than a gallon.　　**True**　**False**

A coffee cup holds less than a gallon.　　**True**　**False**

1 gallon = 4 quarts

2. Which object would be best to measure the weight of a watermelon? (*Circle the correct letter.*)

A.　　　　　　　　　　**B.**

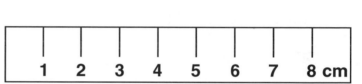

1　2　3　4　5　6　7　8 cm

Name _____ **Date** _____

Warm-Up 56

1. Look at the shape. Write the **area** of the shape.

The shape has an area of _____ square units.

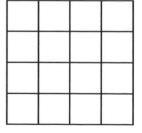

2. Which holds **less** than a quart? (*Circle the correct letter.*)

A. a washing machine

B. a drinking glass

C. a swimming pool

 **=**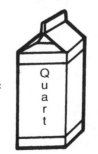

4 cups = 1 quart

DAILY
Warm-Up 57

Name _____   Date _____

1. Match the plane shapes with the correct letter.

triangle   _____

rectangle   _____

square   _____

circle   _____

A.   **C.**

B.    **D.**

2. Match the solid shapes with the correct letter.

cone   _____

rectangular prism _____

sphere   _____

cube   _____

A.   **C.**

B.   **D.**

DAILY
Warm-Up 58

Name _____   Date _____

1. Who drew a shape with the least amount of sides? (*Circle the correct letter.*)

A.   **B.**   **C.**   **D.**

Mark   Jim   Peggy   Joan

2. Use the pig counter to **estimate** the length of the line.

_____   The line = _____ pig counters.

🐷

Name _____ Date _____

1. Which tool is the best to see how tall a drinking glass would be? (*Circle the correct letter.*)

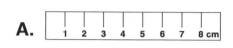 **A.**  **B.** 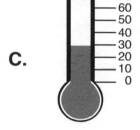 **C.**

2. Which tool is the best to measure temperature? (*Circle the correct letter.*)

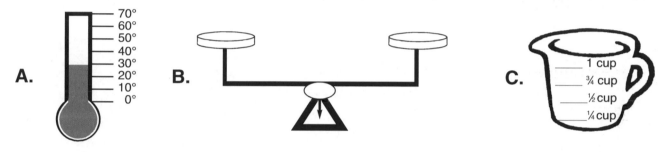

A.   **B.**   **C.**

Name _____ Date _____

1. Draw a circle inside a square. Then, draw a triangle under the square.

2. Circle the letter of the object that is the **longest**.

A.

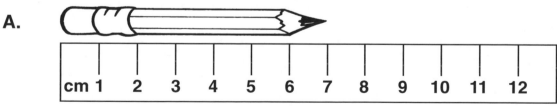

B.

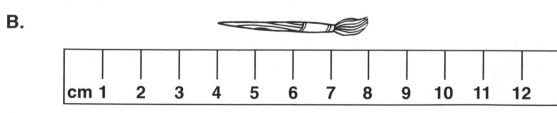

Name _____ **Date** _____

DAILY Warm-Up 61

1. Mark hands on the clock showing **4:30**.

2. Draw a line on each shape showing two equal parts.

   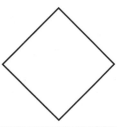

DAILY Warm-Up 62

Name _____ **Date** _____

1. Is this a line of symmetry? (*Circle your answer.*)

Yes

No

2. Circle the letter of the thermometer that probably reads the temperature of a hot summer day.

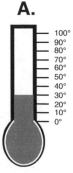

A.   **B.**   **C.**

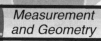
Answer Key

Warm-Up 1
1. D   2. C

Warm-Up 2
1. D   2. No

Warm-Up 3
1. 5   2. A

Warm-Up 4
1. D
2.

Warm-Up 5
1. C
2.
 8:10

Warm-Up 6
1.
2. A. 1:20
   B. 2:25
   C. 3:55
   D. 4:30

Warm-Up 7
1. 8
2. A. 3:45
   B. 9:30
   C. 5:15
   D. 8:20

Warm-Up 8
1. D
2. 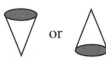 or

Warm-Up 9
1. 4   2. D

Warm-Up 10
1. B
2. A
   C
   B
   D

Warm-Up 11
1. 5   2. C

Warm-Up 12
1. 4   2. C

Warm-Up 13
1. No
2. Ended

Warm-Up 14
1.
2.

Warm-Up 15
1. D   2. A

Warm-Up 16
1. B   2. Yes

Warm-Up 17
1. Stack 2   2. B

Warm-Up 18
1. A   2. 7

Warm-Up 19
1. A   2. 8

Warm-Up 20
1.
2. 8

Warm-Up 21
1. C
2.

Warm-Up 22
1. Sides: 4
   Corners: 4
2.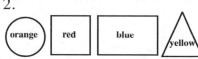

Warm-Up 23
1.
2. A

Warm-Up 24
1.
2. B

Warm-Up 25
1. A   2. 6:05

Warm-Up 26
1.
2. 24 square units
   16 square units

Warm-Up 27
1. B
2.

Warm-Up 28
1. Yes, No, Yes, No
2. No

Warm-Up 29
1. C
2.

Warm-Up 30
1. Friday
2. triangle rectangle circle square

Warm-Up 31
1. car   2. 4

Warm-Up 32
1. envelope
2.

Warm-Up 33
1. Thursday   2. cylinder

Warm-Up 34
1. rectangle = 4 sides
   triangle = 3 sides
2.

Warm-Up 35
1. B   2. Alike

Warm-Up 36
1. B
2. A, B

Warm-Up 37
1. B   2. A

Warm-Up 38
1. Answers will vary.
2. sphere

Warm-Up 39
1. 4   2. False

Warm-Up 40
1. Answers will vary.
2.

Warm-Up 41
1. Yes, No   2. B

Warm-Up 42
1. Sample Answer: One is
   flat shaped, and the other
   is three-dimensional.
2. B

Warm-Up 43
1. C   2. 60, 60

Warm-Up 44
1. A   2. B

Warm-Up 45
1. 6
2. oval, octagon, triangle,
   rectangle

Warm-Up 46
1. B
2. All spheres should be
   colored red.

Warm-Up 47
1. 7   2. 31

Warm-Up 48
1. B   2. C

Warm-Up 49
1. 4   2. B, D, A, C

Warm-Up 50
1. May, 31, Tuesday
2. 12

Warm-Up 51
1. A = 9 cm
   B = 11 cm
2. C

Warm-Up 52
1.

2. 5

Warm-Up 53
1. 2:00   2.

Warm-Up 54
1. False
2.

1:15   1:30

1:45   2:00

Warm-Up 55
1. True
   True
2. A

Warm-Up 56
1. 16   2. B

Warm-Up 57
1. triangle = D
   rectangle = B
   square = A
   circle = C
2. cone = B
   rectangular prism = A
   sphere = D
   cube = C

Warm-Up 58
1. D   2. 4

Warm-Up 59
1. A   2. A

Warm-Up 60
1.
2. A

Warm-Up 61
1.
2. Sample Answers:

Warm-Up 62
1. No   2. B

GRAPHS, DATA AND PROBABILITY

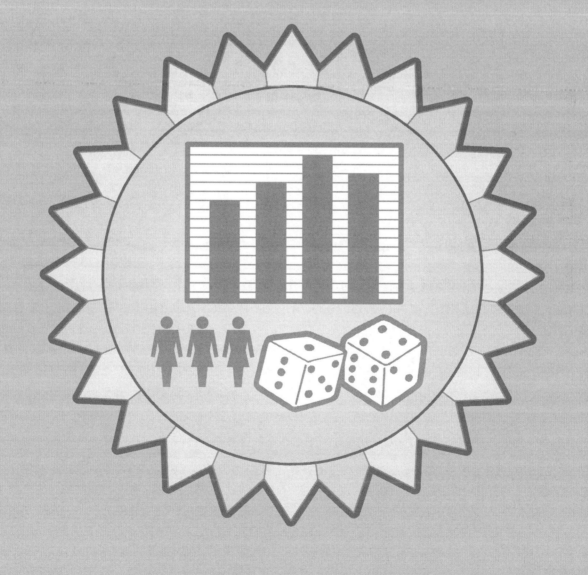

Name _____ **Date** _____

1. Answer the following questions by circling the best answer.

Children don't like candy.   **Likely**   **Not Likely**

Ice melts slowly in freezing weather.   **Likely**   **Not Likely**

2. Who won the **most** games? (*Circle the correct letter.*)

A. Brandi

B. Gordon

Basketball Games Won	
Brandi	🏀 🏀 🏀 🏀
Gordon	🏀 🏀 🏀 🏀 🏀 🏀

- -

Name _____ **Date** _____

1. James asked his friends which pet they liked best. The following tallies are the answers his friends gave. Complete the graph using the marks beside each pet.

Dog   卌 卌

Cat   卌 ||

Hamster   卌

Goldfish |

Favorite Pet

10
9
8
7
6
5
4
3
2
1
0

Dog   Goldfish   Cat   Hamster

2. It is likely the sky will turn green and the grass will turn blue. (*Circle your answer.*)

True   **False**

DAILY Warm-Up 3

Name _____ Date _____

1. Circle *likely* or *not likely* for the sentences below.

During the week, you will stay up late. **Likely   Not Likely**

You will have homework if you get behind in school. **Likely   Not Likely**

2. Mark the correct letter to the following problems. *(The first one is done for you.)*

___**A**___ Today, you will see a bird flying in the sky.

_____ Your parents will let you skip school and sleep all day.

_____ Your teacher will mow your parents' lawn.

_____ You will eat pizza every day for a year.

KEY
A. Likely
B. Not Likely

- -

DAILY Warm-Up 4

Name _____ Date _____

1. Look at the graph. What can you tell about the graph?

Books Read

2. Circle the correct answer.

You will ride a giraffe to school. **Likely   Not Likely**

Your teacher will read a book to the class. **Likely   Not Likely**

DAILY Warm-Up 5

Name _____ Date _____

1. Use the bar graph to answer the questions.

   How many pennies did Allie and
   Jake find together?

   _____

   Who found the most pennies?
   (*Circle the correct letter.*)

   A. Mary and Pete   **B.** Pete and Allie

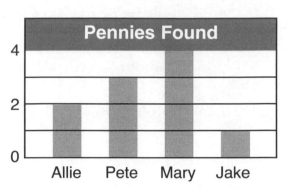

2. On what number will the spinner probably land?

   _____

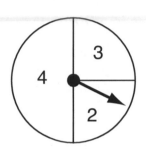

DAILY Warm-Up 6

Name _____ Date _____

1. Use the bar graph to answer the questions below.

   Who read the most pages?

   _____

   Which two students read a total
   of 10 pages?

   _____

   _____

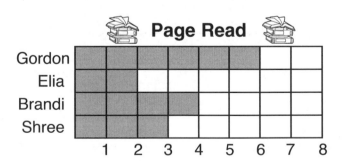

2. Circle *true* or *false*.

   You will likely have homework in school this year.   **True   False**

DAILY Warm-Up 7   Name _____   Date _____

1. Answer the following questions by circling the best answer.

You will ride an elephant to school.   **Likely**   **Not Likely**

You will color a picture in class.   **Likely**   **Not Likely**

2. Ben has 2 cylinders, 3 cubes, and 1 sphere in a bag. If he grabs a shape, which shape will he **least likely** grab? (*Circle the correct letter.*)

A. cylinder   **B.** cube   **C.** sphere

DAILY Warm-Up 8   Name _____   Date _____

1. Terry played baseball with her friends. Complete the graph to show the results.

RESULTS			
Mark	7	Jim	9
Lynn	4	Sue	5

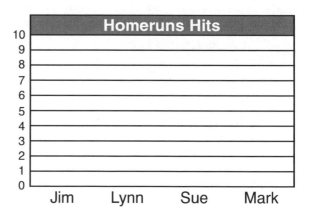

Homeruns Hits

10
9
8
7
6
5
4
3
2
1
0
    Jim   Lynn   Sue   Mark

2. Look at the spinner. On what number will the spinner **least likely** land? _____

Why? _____

_____

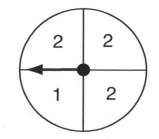

DAILY Warm-Up 9

Name _____   Date _____

1. Circle the best answer.

You will use a pencil at school this week.   **Likely**   **Not Likely**

You will eat 10 apples each day for a week.   **Likely**   **Not Likely**

2. Mary has $3.00. Which item can Mary **NOT** buy?

A. package of pencils

B. scissors

C. comic book

D. book of stickers

Package of Pencils **$2.59**	Scissors **$3.25**	Comic Book **$1.79**	Book of Stickers **$2.10**

DAILY Warm-Up 10

Name _____   Date _____

1. Complete the graph. The first one is done for you.

Margaret	3
Meredith	9
Sarah	8
Cindy	5

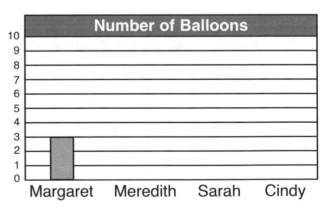

2. Which would you **least likely** do on a winter's day? (*Circle the correct letter.*)

A. build a snowman

B. wear a warm jacket

C. go swimming

DAILY **Warm-Up 11** Name _____ Date _____

1. Look at the spinner. On which color will the spinner **most** likely land?

_____

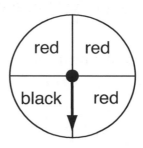

2. Use the graph to answer the questions.

How many does each equal?

_____

How many pictures did Clay take?

_____

 = 2 pictures

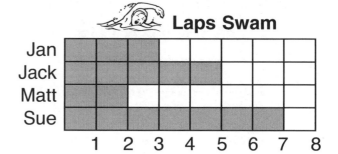

DAILY **Warm-Up 12** Name _____ Date _____

1. Use the bar graph to answer the questions below.

How many laps did Jan and Matt swim?

_____

Who swam the most laps?

_____

 **Laps Swam**

2. Circle the best answer.

You will watch TV this year.   **Likely**   **Not Likely**

Your teacher will ride a zebra to school.   **Likely**   **Not Likely**

DAILY
Warm-Up 13

Name _____ Date _____

1. Circle the best answer.

You will meet new friends at school.　　**Likely**　　**Not Likely**

Your teacher will let you stop doing work in class.　　**Likely**　　**Not Likely**

2. Use the bar graph to answer the questions.

How many students like cats the best?

Students' Favorite Pets

_____

Which pet was most liked?

_____

	Students' Favorite Pets				
Bird 🐦					
Fish 🐟					
Dog 🐕					
Cat 🐈					
	1	2	3	4	5

DAILY
Warm-Up 14

Name _____ Date _____

1. Circle the best answer.

It is likely you will eat pizza this year.　　**True**　　**False**

It is unlikely you will paint your house purple.　　**True**　　**False**

2. What can you tell about the graph?

_____

_____

_____

Books Read	
Pete	📖📖📖📖📖📖
Margo	📖📖📖📖
Janice	📖📖📖📖📖
Debbie	📖📖

DAILY Warm-Up 15

Name _____ Date _____

1. How many home runs did Carrie hit? (*Circle the correct letter.*)

A. 9 **B.** 12 **C.** 24

Number of Home Runs Hit	
Jim	𝍒𝍒 II
Carrie	𝍒𝍒𝍒𝍒 IIII
Linda	𝍒 IIII

2. Use the graph to answer the questions.

How many points did Samantha make?

_____

How many points did Jack and Martha make together?

_____

Points Made Playing Basketball	
Jack	🏀🏀
Samantha	🏀🏀🏀🏀
Martha	🏀🏀🏀🏀🏀🏀

🏀 = 2 points

- -

DAILY Warm-Up 16

Name _____ Date _____

1. Use the picture graph to answer the questions below. (*Circle the correct letter.*)

Which grade read the **most** books?
A. 1st grade
B. 2nd grade
C. 3rd grade

Which grade read exactly 5 books?
A. 1st grade
B. 2nd grade
C. 3rd grade

Books Read	
1st Grade	📖📖📖📖📖📖
2nd Grade	📖📖📖
3rd Grade	📖📖📖📖📖

📖 = 1 book

2. Circle the best answer.

Exercise is good for your health. **True** **False**

It is likely to rain sometime this year. **True** **False**

DAILY Warm-Up 17   Name _____   **Date** _____

1. If these cards were placed in a bag and you grabbed one card without looking, which card would you **most likely** pick? (*Circle the correct letter.*)

| 9 | 2 | 1 | 9 | 9 | 4 | 2 |

A. **9**   B. **1**   C. **2**   D. **4**

2. Use the information below to complete the graph. Shade in one box for every two votes. The first one is done for you.

Yellow	4
Blue	7
Green	9
Red	6

Favorite Color Crayon

Yellow	▨	▨			
Blue					
Green					
Red					

0 2 4 6 8 10
Number of Votes

DAILY Warm-Up 18   Name _____   **Date** _____

1. Circle the best answer.

It is unlikely you will ride a pig to school.   **True**   **False**

It is likely you will learn to ride a bike before you are 30.   **True**   **False**

2. Use the graph to solve the problems.

Who counted the least number of buses?

_____

Who counted two less buses than Maggie?

_____

Number of Buses Counted	
Maggie	🚌 🚌 🚌 🚌 🚌
Beth	🚌 🚌
Hank	🚌 🚌 🚌
Jimmy	🚌 🚌 🚌 🚌

🚌 = 1 bus

Name _____ Date _____

1. Use the tally graph to answer the question.

How many students like the colors green or black best?

Students Favorite Color

Green	𝍸𝍸 𝍸𝍸 𝍸𝍸
Black	𝍸𝍸
Pink	𝍸𝍸 𝍸𝍸
Red	𝍸𝍸 𝍸𝍸 𝍸𝍸 𝍸𝍸 𝍸𝍸

_____ students

2. Circle the sentence that is **most likely** true.

A good education will prepare you for a better life.

It is not important to study before a test.

Name _____ Date _____

1. Circle the sentence that is most likely **NOT** true.

A camel is taller than a giraffe.

An elephant eats more food each day than a wolf.

2. Complete the bar graph using the information provided.

Hamburger	4
Hot Dog	8
Chicken Tenders	6
Pizza	10

Students Favorite Food

```
10
 8
 6
 4
 2
 0
   Hot    Hamburger  Pizza  Chicken
   Dog                      Tenders
```

DAILY
Warm-Up 21

Name _____   Date _____

1. Circle the best answer.

You will find a lost hippopotamus on your way to school.   **Likely**   **Not Likely**

Your pet goldfish will grow to the size of a whale.   **Likely**   **Not Likely**

2. Use the graph to answer the questions.

How many crayons did Jack lose?

_____ crayons

How many crayons did Jack and Sandra lose in all?

_____ crayons

Lost Crayons	
Jack	✏️ ✏️ ✏️ ✏️ ✏️
Sandra	✏️ ✏️

✏️ = 1 crayon

DAILY
Warm-Up 22

Name _____   Date _____

1. How many students like strawberries?

_____ students

Students Who Like Strawberries

Like / Don't Like — 1 2 3 4 5 6 7 8

2. Circle the best answer.

You will wake up, and a tree will be growing in your bedroom.   **Likely**   **Not Likely**

Your teacher will do your homework for a week.   **Likely**   **Not Likely**

DAILY
Warm-Up 23

Name _____ Date _____

1. Which was the **least favorite** food? (*Circle the correct letter.*)

A. hamburger

B. hot dog

C. pizza

Favorite Food Served in the Cafeteria	
Hamburger	🍔🍔🍔🍔🍔🍔
Hot Dog	🌭🌭
Pizza	🍕🍕🍕🍕

2. Use the graph to answer the questions.

How many students liked basketball or football the best?

_____ students

What sport was the favorite sport?

_____

Favorite Sport	
Basketball	🏀🏀🏀🏀🏀🏀
Football	🏈🏈
Tennis	🎾

DAILY
Warm-Up 24

Name _____ Date _____

1. Use the graph to answer the questions below.

What color was liked more than blue?

_____

How many students liked blue or green?

_____

Student Favorite Color	
Blue	B B B B B B B
Red	R R R R R R R R R
Green	G G G G

2. Circle the best answer.

In the summer, it's fun to go swimming. **True** **False**

Your teacher will get mad if you run in the classroom. **True** **False**

DAILY
Warm-Up 25

Name _____ **Date** _____

1. Circle the best answer.

Brushing your teeth is good for you.   **True**   **False**

Vegetables are bad for your health.   **True**   **False**

2. The spinner will most likely land on the color green because . . .

_____

_____

_____

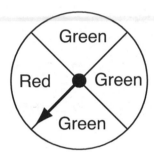

DAILY
Warm-Up 26

Name _____ **Date** _____

1. Use the spinner to answer the problem.

The spinner will most likely land on the number 2. (*Circle your answer.*)

          True   **False**

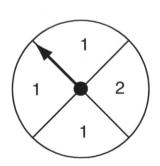

2. Use the graph to answer the questions.

Who read more pages than Mary?

_____

How many pages did Jim and Lynn read together?

_____ pages

Number of Pages Read in a Book			
	📖		
	📖	📖	
📖	📖	📖	
📖	📖	📖	📖
Sam	Jim	Mary	Lynn

DAILY
Warm-Up 27

Name _____   Date _____

1. Use the bar graph to answer the questions.

Who swam the **most** laps?

_____

Who swam the **least** laps?

_____

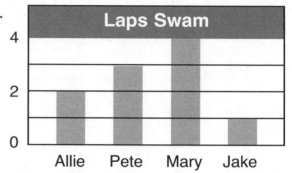

Laps Swam

2. Use the graph to answer the questions.

Which color is the **most** favorite?

_____

Which color is the **least** favorite?

_____

Favorite Color								
Red	R	R	R	R	R	R	R	R
Orange	O	O						
Blue	B	B	B	B	B	B		
Purple	P	P	P	P	P			
Green	G	G	G	G				

DAILY
Warm-Up 28

Name _____   Date _____

1. Use the graph to answer the questions below.

Who read the most books?

_____

Which two students read the same number of books?

_____

_____

Books Read

Sue

Leroy

Agnes

Fannie

2. Circle the best answer.

It is likely pizza will be served in the cafeteria this year.   **True**   **False**

Name _____ **Date** _____

1. Look at the graph. On which number will the spinner most likely land? _____

Why? _____

_____

_____

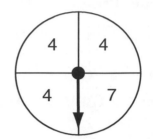

2. Use the graph to answer the questions.

How many does each  equal?

_____ pencils

How many pencils does Ricky have?

_____ pencils

Number of Pencils			
George	✏	✏	✏
Ricky	✏	✏	✏	✏

✏ = 2 pencils

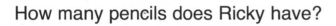

Name _____ **Date** _____

1. Use the bar graph to answer the questions below.

How many miles did Jack ride?

_____ miles

Which two students rode the same number of miles?

_____ and _____

How many miles did Sue ride?

_____ miles

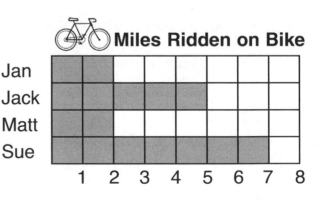

2. Circle the best answer.

Your teacher's pet wolf will eat your lunch.   **Likely**   **Not Likely**

You may get a cold this year.   **Likely**   **Not Likely**

DAILY Warm-Up 31   Name _____   Date _____

1. Who sold the most tickets? (*Circle the correct letter.*)

    A. Linda   **B.** Sarah   **C.** Maggie

Number of Tickets Sold	
Linda	ⵜⵜⵜ ⵜⵜⵜ ||
Sarah	ⵜⵜⵜ ⵜⵜⵜ ⵜⵜⵜ ⵜⵜⵜ ||||
Maggie	ⵜⵜⵜ ||||

2. Use the graph to answer the questions.
How many hours did Stuart practice basketball?

_____ hours

Who practiced the least number
of hours? (*Circle the correct letter.*)

A. Stuart   **B.** Mark   **C.** Jack

Hours Practicing Basketball	
Jack	🏀🏀
Stuart	🏀🏀🏀🏀
Mark	🏀🏀🏀🏀🏀🏀

🏀 = 1 hour

DAILY Warm-Up 32   Name _____   Date _____

1. Use the picture graph to answer the questions below.

Which grade level won the **most** awards?

A. 1st grade **B.** 2nd grade **C.** 3rd grade

Which grade level won six awards?

A. 1st grade **B.** 2nd grade **C.** 3rd grade

Computer Awards Given	
1st Grade	💾💾💾💾
2nd Grade	💾💾
3rd Grade	💾💾💾💾💾💾

2. Circle the best answer.

Running in the classroom will likely get you in trouble. **True**   **False**

You will not get into trouble if you don't do your homework. **True**   **False**

DAILY
Warm-Up 33

Name _____   Date _____

1. Use the tally graph to answer the question.

How many pages did Pete read on Wednesday?

_____ pages

Pages Pete Read	
Monday	~~IIII~~ ~~IIII~~ ~~IIII~~
Tuesday	~~IIII~~
Wednesday	~~IIII~~ ~~IIII~~
Thursday	~~IIII~~ ~~IIII~~ ~~IIII~~ ~~IIII~~ ~~IIII~~

2. Circle the sentence that is most likely **true**.

Studying will help you learn.

Reading books will not teach you anything.

DAILY
Warm-Up 34

Name _____   Date _____

1. Circle the sentence that is most likely **not true**.

A horse can run faster than a cow.

A shark can walk on land.

2. Complete the bar graph using the information provided.

Jack	8
Lou	4
Sam	6
Frank	10

Raffle Tickets Sold

10
8
6
4
2
0

Jack   Lou   Sam   Frank

Name _____   **Date** _____

1. Circle the best answer.

During the winter, you will wear a coat.   **Likely**   **Not Likely**

During the summer, it will snow.   **Likely**   **Not Likely**

2. Why will the spinner most likely land on a bike?

_____

_____

_____

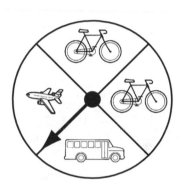

Name _____   **Date** _____

1. Use the spinner to answer the problem. (*Circle your answer.*)

The spinner will most likely land on the letter **G**.

          True   **False**

2. Use the graph to answer the questions.

Who caught more fish than Pat?

_____

Which two students caught a total of 5 fish? (*Circle the correct letter.*)

A. Pat and Lynn

B. Hank and Matt

Number of Fish Caught			
	🐟		
🐟	🐟		
🐟	🐟		🐟
🐟	🐟	🐟	🐟
🐟	🐟	🐟	🐟
Pat	Lynn	Hank	Matt

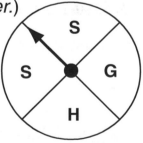

DAILY Warm-Up 37   Name _____   Date _____

1. Use the bar graph to answer the questions.
Who is most likely the best baseball player?

_____

Which two players did **NOT** hit any
home runs? (*Circle the correct letter.*)

A. Mary and Pete   **B.** Sam and Kate

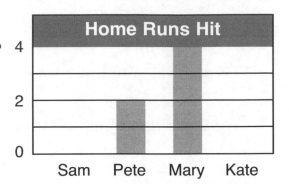

Home Runs Hit

2. Use the graph to answer the questions.
Which number is the **most** favorite?

_____

Which two numbers were the **least**
favorite? (*Circle the correct letter.*)

A. eight and five   **B.** nine and four

Favorite Number							
Eight	8	8	8	8	8		
Five	5	5	5	5	5	5	5
Nine	9	9	9				
Seven	7	7	7	7	7	7	
Four	4	4	4	4			

DAILY Warm-Up 38   Name _____   Date _____

1. Use the picture graph to answer the questions below.

Who earned the **most** computer time?

_____

Which two students earned the
least amount of computer time?
(*Circle the correct letter.*)

A. Agnes and Fannie

B. Sue and Leroy

Computer Time						
Sue	💻	💻				
Leroy	💻					
Agnes	💻	💻	💻			
Fannie	💻	💻	💻	💻		

2. Circle your answer.

It is likely you will make a new friend at school this year.   **True**   **False**

DAILY Warm-Up 39

Name _____ Date _____

1. If you drop a penny, it will land on heads or tails. (*Circle your answer.*)

True   False

2. If you reach into the bag without looking, which shape will you **most likely** pick? (*Circle the correct letter.*)

A.   **B.**   **C.**

DAILY Warm-Up 40

Name _____ Date _____

1. Use the graph to answer the questions.

Which two students wrote the **least** number of letters? (*Circle the correct letter.*)

A. Gordon and Lee

B. Gordon and James

Who wrote the **most** letters?

_____

Letter Wrote to Pen Pal	
Gordon	▫▫▫▫
Lee	▫▫▫▫▫▫▫
Cody	▫▫▫▫▫▫▫▫
James	▫▫▫▫▫

2. On what name will the spinner **most likely** land?

_____

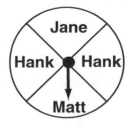

DAILY Warm-Up 41

Name _____ Date _____

1. Circle the best answer.

Your teacher will teach you about math. **Likely**   **Not Likely**

You will get sick and miss a day of school. **Likely**   **Not Likely**

2. Write the correct letter. The first one is done for you.

___A___ You will make at least 50% on a test.

_____ You will not learn math in school.

_____ You will eat a piece of fruit this year.

_____ You will take a bath with a whale.

KEY
A. Likely
B. Not Likely

DAILY Warm-Up 42

Name _____ Date _____

1. Look at the graph. What can you tell about the graph?

I can tell _____

_____

_____

_____

Balloons Popped at Fair

	1	2	3	4	5	6	7	8
Sam	▓	▓	▓	▓	▓			
Lou	▓	▓	▓	▓	▓	▓		
Matt	▓	▓						
Hank	▓	▓	▓	▓	▓	▓	▓	

2. Circle the best answer.

It is likely you will miss two months during the school year.   **True**   **False**

DAILY Warm-Up 43   Name _____ Date _____

1. Circle *likely* or *unlikely*.

On a freezing cold day, you will go swimming in a pond.   **Likely**   **Not Likely**

On a hot summer day, you will wear a heavy coat.   **Likely**   **Not Likely**

2. Circle *likely* or *unlikely*.

On a hot summer day, you will go for a swim.   **Likely**   **Not Likely**

On a cold winter's day, you can build a snowman outside.   **Likely**   **Not Likely**

DAILY Warm-Up 44   Name _____ Date _____

1. Circle *likely* or *unlikely*.

You will go to college after first grade.   **Likely**   **Not Likely**

You will go fishing in a pond and catch a shark.   **Likely**   **Not Likely**

2. Circle *true* or *false*.

It is unlikely you will pass to second grade.   **True**   **False**

It is likely you will get a car for Christmas.   **True**   **False**

It is unlikely you will grow over the summer.   **True**   **False**

It is likely your eyes will change color.   **True**   **False**

It is unlikely you will make new friends this year.   **True**   **False**

DAILY Warm-Up 45 Name _____ Date _____

1. Use the bar graph to answer the questions. (*Circle the correct letter.*)

Of which color car were there the **most**?

A. green   **B.** blue   **C.** red

Of which color car were there the **least**?

A. yellow   **B.** green   **C.** red

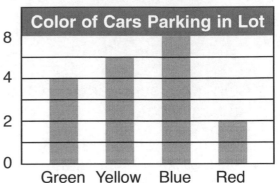

Color of Cars Parking in Lot

(bar graph with values 8, 4, 2, 0; categories: Green, Yellow, Blue, Red)

2. Which is **true** about the spinner?
(*Circle the correct letter.*)

A. It is most likely you will land on a 2.

B. It is most likely you will land on a 3.

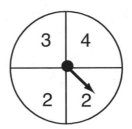

(spinner divided into quarters: 3, 4, 2, 2)

DAILY Warm-Up 46 Name _____ Date _____

1. Complete the graph using the information below. Shade one square with your pencil for each mark.

Raffle Tickets Sold	
Jenn	~~IIII~~
Jeff	~~IIII~~ I
Joy	~~IIII~~ II
Jane	IIII

Raffle Tickets Sold

(blank grid graph with values 0–7; categories: Jeff, Jane, Joy, Jenn)

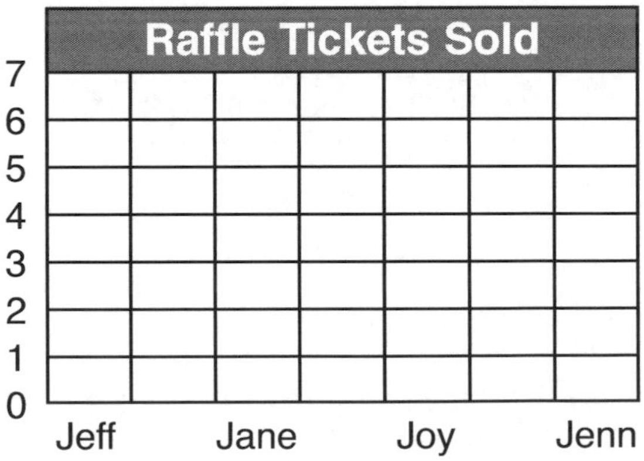

2. If you grab one card without looking, which card will you **most likely** pick?
(*Circle the correct letter.*)

A. Number 3

B. Number 2

C. Number 9

(cards: 9, 2, 3, 2, 9, 9)

DAILY Warm-Up 47

Name _____ Date _____

1. Answer the following questions by circling the best answer.

My teacher will likely paint his or her hair orange. **Likely** **Not Likely**

This year I will read a book. **Likely** **Not Likely**

2. On what will the spinner **most likely** land? (*Circle the correct letter.*)

A.    C. ✈

B. 🚲   D. ☎

DAILY Warm-Up 48

Name _____ Date _____

1. Complete the bar graph to show the results below.

RESULTS	
Orange	2
Red	7
Blue	10
Green	4

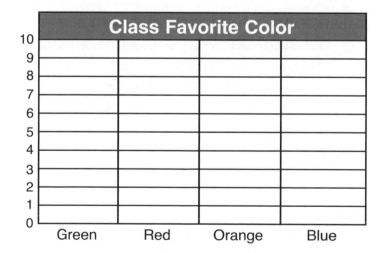

Class Favorite Color

10 9 8 7 6 5 4 3 2 1 0

Green   Red   Orange   Blue

2. Circle *true* or *false*.

Eating too many sweets will likely cause cavities. **True** **False**

Working hard in school will help you make better grades. **True** **False**

DAILY
Warm-Up 49

Name _____ Date _____

1. On what number will the spinner **most likely** land?
(*Circle the correct letter.*)

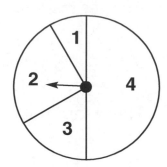

A. 1   **C.** 3

B. 2   **D.** 4

2. Use the graph to answer the questions. (*Circle the correct letter.*)

Who used the most pencils?

A. Jody

B. Sandra

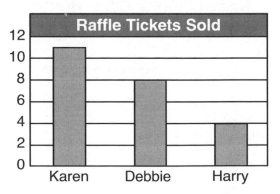

DAILY
Warm-Up 50

Name _____ Date _____

1. Use the bar graph to answer the
question below. (*Circle the correct letter.*)

Which student sold more tickets than
Harry but less than Karen?

A. Karen   **B.** Debbie   **C.** Harry

2. Answer the problems about what might happen during a regular school day.
Circle *likely* or *not likely*.

Your teacher will do your homework.   **Likely**   **Not Likely**

The principal will mow your lawn.   **Likely**   **Not Likely**

DAILY
Warm-Up 51

Name _____ Date _____

1. Use the bar graph to answer the questions. (*Circle the correct letter.*)

How many students were absent in February?

A. 5   **B.** 8   **C.** 7

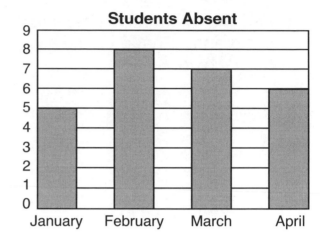

Students Absent

2. Which spinner will **most likely** land on a 4? (*Circle the correct letter.*)

A.    **B.**    **C.**

- -

DAILY
Warm-Up 52

Name _____ Date _____

1. Use the bar graph to answer the question below. (*Circle the correct letter.*)

How many butterflies were seen in June and July?

A. 5

B. 8

C. 10

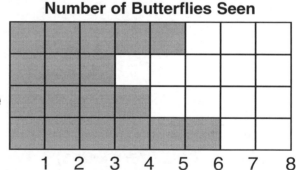

Number of Butterflies Seen

2. Which number will **most likely** be next in the pattern? (*Write it on the line.*)

8, 8, 8, 3, 2, 1, 8, 8, 8, 3, 2, 1, _____

DAILY
Warm-Up 53

Name _____   Date _____

1. Use the information below to complete the graph. Shade in one square for each vote.

Red	4
Green	7
Yellow	8
Blue	6
Orange	5

Votes For Favorite Color								
Red								
Green								
Yellow								
Blue								
Orange								
	1	2	3	4	5	6	7	8

Number of Votes

2. Circle *likely* or *not likely*.

A dog weighs more than an elephant.   **Likely**   **Not Likely**

If you roll a die, it may land on a 7.   **Likely**   **Not Likely**

Your dog will learn to fly.   **Likely**   **Not Likely**

DAILY
Warm-Up 54

Name _____   Date _____

1. Which letter will **most likely** be next in the pattern? (*Write it on the line.*)

A, A, A, B, C, A, A, A, _____

2. Use the graph to solve the problem. (*Circle the correct letter.*)

Of which flower were there more planted?

A. Rose   **B.** Lily   **C.** Tulip

Flowers Planted	
Rose	🌸🌸🌸🌸🌸🌸🌸
Lily	🌸🌸🌸
Tulip	🌸🌸🌸🌸

🌸 = 2 flowers

DAILY **Warm-Up 55**   Name _____   Date _____

1. On what letter will the spinner **least likely** land? (*Circle the correct letter.*)

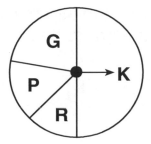

A. G   **C.** R

B. P   **D.** K

2. Which card will **most likely** be next in the pattern? (*Circle the correct letter.*)

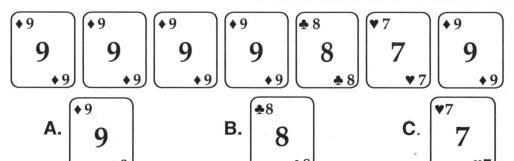

A. [♦9 / 9 / ♦9]   **B.** [♣8 / 8 / ♣8]   **C.** [♥7 / 7 / ♥7]

DAILY **Warm-Up 56**   Name _____   Date _____

1. Use the bar graph to answer the questions below. (*Circle the correct letter.*)

Who used more sheets of paper than Hank but less than Mary?

A. Mary   **B.** Hank   **C.** Joey

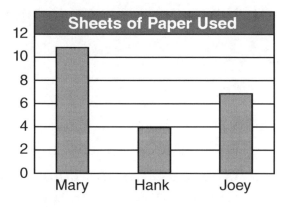

2. Circle the best answer.

You will eat 100 apples for breakfast.   **Likely**   **Not Likely**

You will not eat an apple today.   **Likely**   **Not Likely**

DAILY Warm-Up 57

Name _____ **Date** _____

1. Use the information to complete the bar graph.

 ||||  ||||||| ||||||

 |||||| ||| ♀ |||||| |

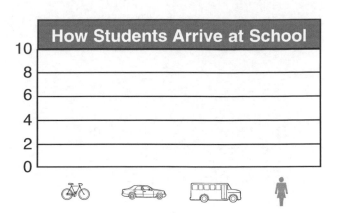

How Students Arrive at School

10
8
6
4
2
0

2. Circle the best answer.

All children know how to swim. **True** **False**

Children never sleep late on the weekend. **True** **False**

DAILY Warm-Up 58

Name _____ **Date** _____

1. Which letter is **most likely** next in the pattern? (*Circle the correct letter.*)

A. G   **B.** H   **C.** F

GHFGHFGH _____

2. Use the bar graph to answer the question below. (*Circle the correct letter.*) Of which type of vehicle were there more?

A. SUV and Van

B. SUV and Truck

C. SUV and Car

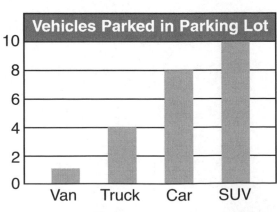

Vehicles Parked in Parking Lot

10
8
6
4
2
0

Van   Truck   Car   SUV

DAILY
Warm-Up 59

Name _____ Date _____

1. Use the information below to complete the graph.

Yellow	7
Blue	4
Red	6
Green	5
Orange	8

Name of Color Candy								
Yellow								
Blue								
Red								
Green								
Orange								
	1	2	3	4	5	6	7	8

2. Circle *true* or *false*.

It is unlikely that you will learn to fly.   **True**   **False**

It is likely you will never use a computer.   **True**   **False**

DAILY
Warm-Up 60

Name _____ Date _____

1. Circle *true* or *false*.

It is likely an elephant can take a bath in 1 gallon of water.   **True**   **False**

It is unlikely a whale can live in 5 gallons of water.   **True**   **False**

2. Use the graph to answer the question. (*Circle the correct letter.*)

How many students have brown eyes?

A. 8

B. 12

C. 30

Student Eye Color	
Blue	👁 👁 👁 👁
Brown	👁 👁 👁 👁 👁 👁
Green	👁 👁 👁
Blue/Green	👁 👁

👁 = 2 children

Name _____ Date _____

1. Who won more video games than Jackson but less than Marshal? (*Circle the correct letter.*)

A. Jackson

B. Marshal

C. Cindy

Video Games Won	
Jackson	𝍷𝍷𝍷𝍷𝍷 𝍷𝍷𝍷𝍷𝍷 𝍷𝍷
Marshal	𝍷𝍷𝍷𝍷𝍷 𝍷𝍷𝍷𝍷𝍷 𝍷𝍷𝍷𝍷𝍷 𝍷𝍷𝍷𝍷𝍷 𝍷𝍷𝍷𝍷
Cindy	𝍷𝍷𝍷𝍷𝍷 𝍷𝍷𝍷𝍷𝍷 𝍷𝍷𝍷𝍷

2. Use the graph to answer the questions. (*Circle the correct letter.*)

How many stickers did Vivian and Pete collect?

A. 5   **B.** 8   **C.** 13

Stickers Collected	
Pete	☺☺☺☺☺☺☺☺
Martha	☺☺☺☺☺☺☺☺☺☺
Vivian	☺☺☺☺☺

☺ = 1 sticker

Name _____ Date _____

1. Use the graph to answer the question below. (*Circle the correct letter.*)

How many students were on the honor roll in first grade?

A. 7

B. 4

C. 9

Number of Honor Roll Students	
1st Grade	AAAAAAAAA
2nd Grade	AAAA
3rd Grade	AAAAAAA

A = 1 student

2. Circle *true* or *false*.

It is likely your teacher will read a book to the class.   **True**   **False**

It is likely you will have recess all day.   **True**   **False**

Graphs, Data and Probability

Answer Key

Warm-Up 1
1. Not Likely
   Not Likely
2. B

Warm-Up 2
1.

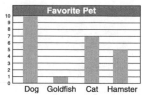

2. False

Warm-Up 3
1. Not Likely, Likely
2. A, B, B, B

Warm-Up 4
1. Answers will vary.
2. Not Likely
   Likely

Warm-Up 5
1. 3 pennies   2. 4
   A

Warm-Up 6
1. Gordon
   Gordon and Brandi
2. True

Warm-Up 7
1. Not Likely   2. C
   Likely

Warm-Up 8
1.

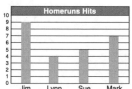

2. 1, It will least likely land on the number 1 because there are more number 2s on the spinner.

Warm-Up 9
1. Likely   2. B
   Not Likely

Warm-Up 10
1.

Number of Balloons			

(bar graph: Margaret, Meredith, Sarah, Cindy)

2. C

Warm-Up 11
1. red   2. 2 pictures
                   8 pictures

Warm-Up 12
1. 5 laps   2. Likely
   Sue   Not Likely

Warm-Up 13
1. Likely   2. 3 students
   Not Likely   Dog

Warm-Up 14
1. True
   True
2. Answers will vary.

Warm-Up 15
1. C
2. 8 points, 16 points

Warm-Up 16
1. A   2. True
   C   True

Warm-Up 17
1. A
2.

Favorite Color Crayon					
Yellow					
Blue					
Green					
Red					
0	2	4	6	8	10

Number of Votes

Warm-Up 18
1. True   2. Beth
   True   Hank

Warm-Up 19
1. 20 students
2. A good education will prepare you for a better life.

Warm-Up 20
1. A camel is taller than a giraffe.
2.

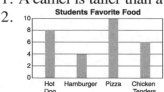

Warm-Up 21
1. Not Likely   2. 5 crayons
   Not Likely   7 crayons

Warm-Up 22
1. 7 students   2. Not Likely
                   Not Likely

Warm-Up 23
1. B   2. 8 students
                   basketball

Warm-Up 24
1. red   2. True
   11 students   True

Warm-Up 25
1. True
   False
2. There are more "Green" spaces on the spinner.

Warm-Up 26
1. False   2. Jim
                   5 pages

Warm-Up 27
1. Mary   2. red
   Jake   orange

Warm-Up 28
1. Fannie
   Sue and Agnes
2. True

Warm-Up 29
1. 4, There are more spaces for the number 4.
2. 2 pencils
   8 pencils

Warm-Up 30
1. 5 miles   2. Not Likely
   Jan and Matt   Likely
   7 miles

Graphs, Data and Probability

Answer Key

Warm-Up 31
1. B
2. 4 hours
   C

Warm-Up 32
1. C
   C
2. True
   False

Warm-Up 33
1. 10 pages
2. Studying will help you learn.

Warm-Up 34
1. A shark can walk on land.
2.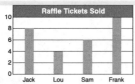

Warm-Up 35
1. Likely
   Not Likely
2. There are more bike spaces.

Warm-Up 36
1. False
2. Lynn
   B

Warm-Up 37
1. Mary
   B
2. 5
   B

Warm-Up 38
1. Fannie
   B
2. True

Warm-Up 39
1. True
2. A

Warm-Up 40
1. B
   Cody
2. Hank

Warm-Up 41
1. Likely
   Likely
2. A
   B
   A
   B

Warm-Up 42
1. Answers will vary.
2. False

Warm-Up 43
1. Not Likely
   Not Likely
2. Likely
   Likely

Warm-Up 44
1. Not Likely
   Not Likely
2. False
   False
   False
   False
   False

Warm-Up 45
1. B
   C
2. A

Warm-Up 46
1.
2. C

Warm-Up 47
1. Not Likely
   Likely
2. C

Warm-Up 48
1.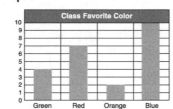
2. True
   True

Warm-Up 49
1. D
2. A

Warm-Up 50
1. B
2. Not Likely
   Not Likely

Warm-Up 51
1. B
2. C

Warm-Up 52
1. C
2. 8

Warm-Up 53
1.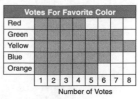
2. Not Likely
   Not Likely
   Not Likely

Warm-Up 54
1. B
2. A

Warm-Up 55
1. C
2. A

Warm-Up 56
1. C
2. Not Likely
   Likely

Warm-Up 57
1.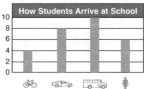
2. False
   False

Warm-Up 58
1. C
2. C

Warm-Up 59
1.
2. True
   False

Warm-Up 60
1. False
   True
2. B

Warm-Up 61
1. C
2. C

Warm-Up 62
1. C
2. True
   False

ALGEBRA, PATTERNS AND FUNCTIONS

DAILY
Warm-Up 1

Name _____ Date _____

1. Complete each table. The first is done for you.

+ 4	
4	8
6	10
8	12
10	14

+ 3	
2	
3	
4	
5	

+ 2	
3	
4	
5	
6	

2. Write the next three numbers in the pattern.

1st	2nd	3rd	4th	5th	6th
2	4	6			

DAILY
Warm-Up 2

Name _____ Date _____

1. Which pattern is shown below? (*Circle the correct letter.*)

A. ABCABC

B. ABBCABBC

C. ABCDABCD

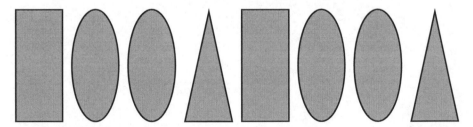

2. Look at the pattern below. Which answer shows the pattern? (*Circle the correct letter.*)

A B C D A B C D

144

Name _____ **Date** _____

1. Look at the pattern of numbers. Write the next two numbers in each pattern.

A.　3,　6,　9,　12,　_____,　_____

B.　4,　3,　2,　1,　4,　3,　_____,　_____

C.　5,　10,　15,　20,　_____,　_____

2. What comes next in the pattern? (*Circle the correct letter.*)

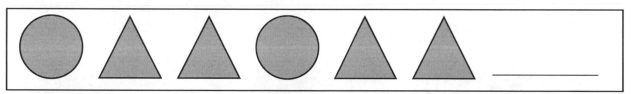

A. 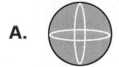　　　**B.** 　　　**C.**

Name _____ **Date** _____

1. Look at the pattern below. Which shapes come next in the pattern? (*Circle the correct letter.*)

A.

B.

C.

2. Draw the next shapes in the pattern.

A.  _____　_____

B.  _____　_____

Name _____ **Date** _____

1. Look at the pattern of shapes. Which answer continues the pattern? (*Circle the correct letter.*)

A. ☐○△△☐○   **B.** ○△△☐○☐   **C.** △△☐○△△

2. Continue the pattern.

ABBABBA ___ ___

- -

Name _____ **Date** _____

1. Complete the chart. What pattern do you see?

_____

_____

_____

_____

Number of Toes			
1 person = __10__ toes		5 people = _____ toes	
2 people = _____ toes		6 people = _____ toes	
3 people = _____ toes		7 people = _____ toes	
4 people = _____ toes		8 people = _____ toes	

2. Name the pattern. (*Circle the correct letter.*)

| **1** | **1** | **2** | **2** | **1** | **1** | **2** | **2** |

A. ABBCAABC   **B.** AABBAABB   **C.** ABCABCAB

Name _____ **Date** _____

DAILY Warm-Up 7

1. Write your answers in the boxes.

A. 1 + 3 = 2 + ☐   **D.** 2 + 1 = 0 + ☐   **G.** 0 + 4 = 3 + ☐

B. 4 + 1 = 5 + ☐   **E.** 3 + 3 = 5 + ☐   **H.** 3 + 3 = 4 + ☐

C. 2 + 0 = 0 + ☐   **F.** 5 + 2 = 6 + ☐   **I.** 3 + 1 = 2 + ☐

2. Write the number that continues the pattern.

9 8 7 9 8 7 9 8 7 ____

Name _____ **Date** _____

DAILY Warm-Up 8

1. Write the number that completes the table.

IN	OUT
1	2
2	3
3	

2. Answer the problems below.

A. 1 + 2 = 3 + ☐   **D.** 2 + 1 = 3 + ☐   **G.** 3 + 2 = 4 + ☐

B. 3 + 1 = 4 + ☐   **E.** 3 + 2 = 5 + ☐   **H.** 0 + 2 = 2 + ☐

C. 0 + 5 = 5 + ☐   **F.** 5 + 2 = 6 + ☐   **I.** 1 + 1 = 2 + ☐

DAILY Warm-Up 9

Name _____ Date _____

1. Which card would be next in the pattern? (*Circle the correct letter.*)

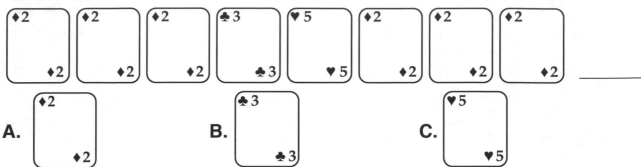

A. **B.** **C.**

2. Write the number that makes the problem true.

$$3 + \boxed{} = 2 + 4$$

DAILY Warm-Up 10

Name _____ Date _____

1. Draw what comes next in the pattern. (*Circle the correct letter.*)

2. Which card comes next in the pattern? (*Circle the correct letter.*)

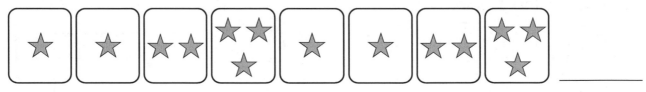

A. **B.** **C.**

DAILY Warm-Up 11   Name _____   Date _____

1. Copy the dots that will complete the pattern on the blank domino.

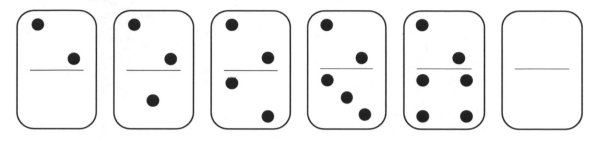

2. Use the numbers 2, 3, and 5 to write four number sentences.

_____ + _____ = _____   _____ − _____ = _____

_____ + _____ = _____   _____ − _____ = _____

DAILY Warm-Up 12   Name _____   Date _____

1. Complete each table. Use the example as your guide.

Example

+ 2	
2	4
3	5
4	6

+ 2	
4	
5	
6	

+ 3	
5	
6	
7	

+ 4	
1	
2	
3	

2. Name the pattern.

Blue, Blue, Red, Green, Blue, Blue, Red, Green

_____

Name _____ **Date** _____

1. Solve the problem.

$$2 + 1 = 3 + \boxed{}$$

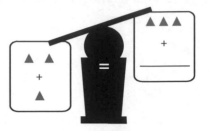

What missing number will balance the scale?

2. Solve the problem.

$$\boxed{} + 3 = 5 + 1$$

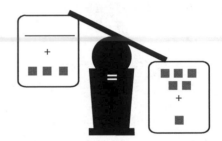

What missing number will balance the scale?

Name _____ **Date** _____

1. Solve the problem.

$$2 + 3 = \boxed{} + 4$$

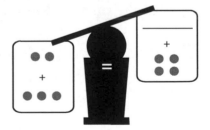

2. What is missing in the pattern? (*Circle the correct letter.*)

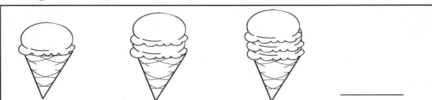

A.   **B.**   **C.**

DAILY
Warm-Up 15

Name _____ **Date** _____

1. Draw what will come next in the pattern.

_____

2. Use the numbers 8, 6, and 2 to write four number sentences.

_____ + _____ = _____   _____ – _____ = _____

_____ + _____ = _____   _____ – _____ = _____

DAILY
Warm-Up 16

Name _____ **Date** _____

1. Name the pattern.

6   6   ♥   ★   6   6   ♥   ★

_____

2. Draw an **ABCABC** pattern.

Name _____ **Date** _____

1. Look at the number pattern. Write the numbers that come next in the pattern.

12, 22, 32, 42, ____, ____, ____

2. What rule is used in the pattern below?

12, 15, 14, 17, 16, 19

The rule for this pattern is: _____

Name _____ **Date** _____

1. Draw the shape that comes next in the pattern.

____

2. Which answer shows the pattern of shapes? (*Circle the correct letter.*)

A. ABBABC   **B.** ABBABB

Name _____ **Date** _____

1. Write the number that is missing.

$$9 - y = 5$$

$y =$ _____

2. Write four number sentences using 5, 9, and 14.

_____ + _____ = _____   _____ − _____ = _____

_____ + _____ = _____   _____ − _____ = _____

Name _____ **Date** _____

1. Find the missing numbers.

$$5 + \underline{\qquad} = 12$$

$$8 + \underline{\qquad} = 14$$

2. What number makes the equation true?

$$12 + \underline{\qquad} = 7 + 5$$

Algebra, Patterns and Functions

DAILY Warm-Up 21

Name _____ **Date** _____

1. Solve the problem.

$$4 + 6 = 4 + \boxed{}$$

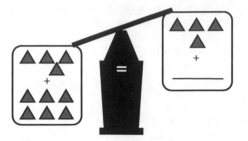

What missing number will balance the scale?

2. Solve the problem.

$$\boxed{} + 4 = 6 + 5$$

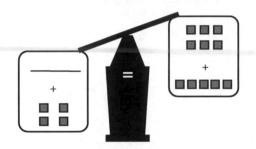

What missing number will balance the scale?

Algebra, Patterns and Functions

DAILY Warm-Up 22

Name _____ **Date** _____

1. Solve the problem.

$$2 + 10 = \boxed{} + 5$$

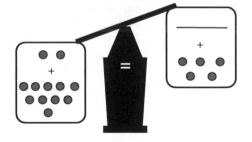

What missing number will balance the scale?

2. What is missing in the pattern? (*Circle the correct letter.*)

A.   **B.**   **C.**

#3959 Daily Warm-Ups: Math   154   ©Teacher Created Resources, Inc.

1. Write four number sentences about the envelopes.

_____ + _____ = _____

_____ + _____ = _____

_____ – _____ = _____

_____ – _____ = _____

2. Solve the problem below.

$$6 + \boxed{} = 4 + 4$$

----

1. Write four number sentences about the shapes.

_____ + _____ = _____

_____ + _____ = _____

_____ – _____ = _____

_____ – _____ = _____

2. What is happening to the numbers below?

IN	1	2	3	4	5	6
OUT	2	3	4	5	6	7

_____

_____

Name _____ **Date** _____

Warm-Up 25

1. Which card would be next in the pattern? (*Circle the correct letter.*)

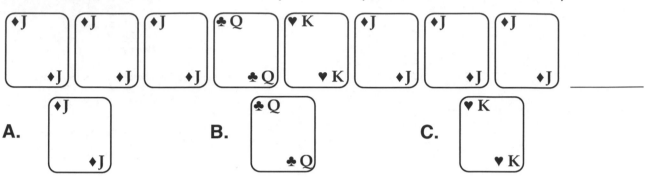

A. ♦J / ♦J   **B.** ♣Q / ♣Q   **C.** ♥K / ♥K

2. Write the number that would make the problem true.

$$12 + \boxed{} = 9 + 11$$

Name _____ **Date** _____

Warm-Up 26

1. If 11 is put in the "IN" column, what number will be put in the "OUT" column? (*Circle the correct letter.*)

IN	6	7	8	9	10	11
OUT	8	9	10	11	12	

A. 12   **B.** 13   **C.** 14

2. Complete the pattern of numbers in the boxes below.

2	4	6	8		12	14	

DAILY Warm-Up 27 Name _____ Date _____

1. Look at the pattern of numbers. Write what comes next in the pattern.

2,   4,   6,   _____,   _____

2. Look at the pattern. Draw the missing two shapes.

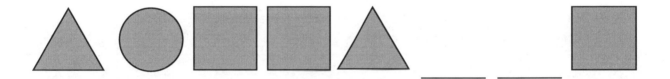

DAILY Warm-Up 28 Name _____ Date _____

1. Look at the pattern below. Which shape comes next in the pattern? (*Circle the correct letter.*)

A. 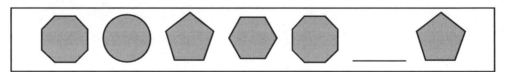   B.   C.   D.

2. Solve the problem.

$$6 + w = 13$$

$$w = \text{_____}$$

Name _____   Date _____

Warm-Up 29

1. Look at the table. If the pattern continues, how many pages will Carrie read on Thursday? (*Fill in the empty box.*)

Pages Read	
Monday	2
Tuesday	4
Wednesday	6
Thursday	

2. What comes next in the pattern? (*Circle the correct letter.*)

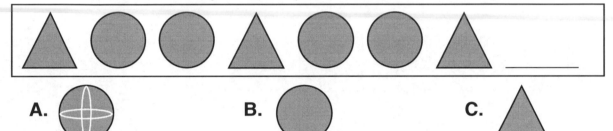

A. ⊕   **B.** ●   **C.** ▲

Name _____   Date _____

Warm-Up 30

1. Look at the pattern below. Which shape comes next in the pattern? (*Circle the correct letter.*)

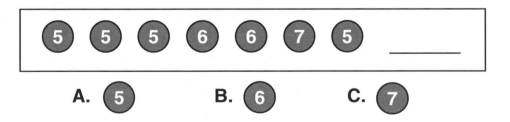

A. ⑤   **B.** ⑥   **C.** ⑦

2. Solve the problem.

$$9 + \_\_\_\_\_ = 18$$

The missing number is _____.

DAILY Warm-Up 31

Name _____ Date _____

1. Look at the pattern. Color the blank circle to continue the pattern.

Color **Y** circles yellow. | yellow |

Color **G** circles green. | green |

2. Draw the dots on the blank domino that will complete the pattern.

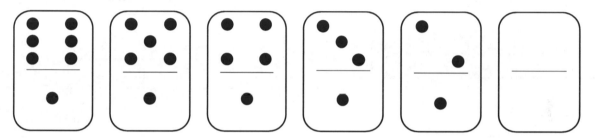

DAILY Warm-Up 32

Name _____ Date _____

1. Write the number that is missing in the pattern.

10, 12, _____, 16, 18

2. Continue the pattern.

A, A, B, B, C, C, D, D, E, E, F, _____

Name _____ **Date** _____

1. Write the number that comes next in the pattern.

6, 2, 2, 5, 6, 2, 2, 5, _____

2. Look at the table. If the number 5 is put "IN," what number will come "OUT"?

IN	2	3	4	5
OUT	4	5	6	

Name _____ **Date** _____

Warm-Up 34

1. Fill in the missing numbers to show equal values.

4 + _____ = 3 + 9

5 + 5 = 6 + _____

2. Circle *true* or *false* to the problems below.

2 + $\boxed{3}$ = 4 + 2   **True**   **False**

3 + $\boxed{5}$ = 8 + 1   **True**   **False**

Name _____ **Date** _____

1. What number goes in the empty space? (*Circle the correct letter.*)

| 6 6 4 3 6 6 4 3 ____ |

A. 6   **B.** 4   **C.** 3

2. Circle the letter of the missing number that makes the pattern true.

| 10, 15, 20, ____ , 30 |

A. 20   **B.** 25   **C.** 30

- -

Name _____ **Date** _____

1. Fill in the missing number that makes the problem true.

$$8 + \underline{\quad} = 2 + 14$$

2. Fill in the missing number in the pattern below.

IN	1	2	3	4
OUT	4	5	6	

Name _____ **Date** _____

Warm-Up 37

1. Look at the pattern of shaded numbers on the hundred chart. What is being done?

_____

_____

_____

1	2	3	4	5	6	7	8	9	10
11	12	13	14	15	16	17	18	19	20
21	22	23	24	25	26	27	28	29	30
31	32	33	34	35	36	37	38	39	40
41	42	43	44	45	46	47	48	49	50
51	52	53	54	55	56	57	58	59	60
61	62	63	64	65	66	67	68	69	70
71	72	73	74	75	76	77	78	79	80
81	82	83	84	85	86	87	88	89	90
91	92	93	94	95	96	97	98	99	100

2. Which number makes the problem true? (*Circle the correct letter.*)

A. 4

B. 5

C. 6

D. 7

$$7 + 7 = 9 + \underline{}$$

Name _____ **Date** _____

Warm-Up 38

1. Look at the pattern. Circle the shape that continues the pattern.

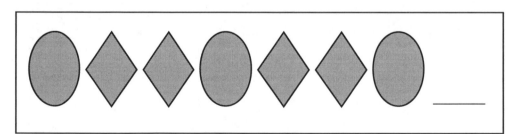 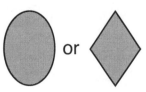

2. What answer names the pattern? (*Circle the correct letter.*)

A. ABCDABCD

B. ABCCABCD

C. ABCCABCC

Name _____ **Date** _____

1. Fill in the missing numbers in the pattern below.

10, 15, 20, 25, _____ , _____ , _____

2. Complete the pattern Sammy wrote.

1	3	5	7	9	11
	15	17	19		23
25		29	31	33	

Name _____ **Date** _____

1. Continue the pattern below.

4, 8, 12, 16, _____ , _____

2. Continue the pattern of numbers in the boxes below.

2	5	8		14	17	20	

DAILY **Name** _____ **Date** _____
Warm-Up 41

1. What shape goes in the empty space? (*Circle the correct letter.*)

A. ◻

B. △

C. ○

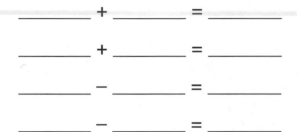

2. Look at the domino. Write the fact families.

_____ + _____ = _____

_____ + _____ = _____

_____ − _____ = _____

_____ − _____ = _____

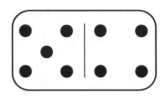

DAILY **Name** _____ **Date** _____
Warm-Up 42

1. Fill in the missing number that makes each problem true.

A. $9 + \underline{\quad} = 14 + 2$ **C.** $\underline{\quad} + 3 = 4 + 4$

B. $7 + 5 = 12 + \underline{\quad}$ **D.** $3 + 4 = \underline{\quad} + 1$

2. What is the next number in the pattern? (*Circle the correct letter.*)

A. 6

B. 7

C. 8

6, 6, 7, 8, 6, 6, 7, _____

DAILY **Warm-Up 43** Name _____ Date _____

1. Look at the table. If the pattern continues, how many laps will Jennifer swim on Monday?

Laps Swam	
Friday	3
Saturday	6
Sunday	9
Monday	

2. What shape comes next in the pattern? (*Circle the correct letter.*)

A.   **B.**   **C.**

DAILY **Warm-Up 44** Name _____ Date _____

1. Look at the pattern in the box. Which shapes come next in the pattern? (*Circle the correct letter.*)

A.

B.

C.

2. Solve the problems.

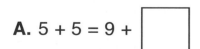

A. $5 + 5 = 9 + \boxed{}$ **C.** $5 + 10 = 6 + \boxed{}$ **E.** $9 + 9 = 7 + \boxed{}$

B. $9 + 3 = 6 + \boxed{}$ **D.** $7 + 6 = 9 + \boxed{}$ **F.** $6 + 3 = 2 + \boxed{}$

DAILY Warm-Up 45

Name _____ Date _____

1. Look at the number pattern below. Write the number that goes in the empty box.

3	6	9	12		18

2. Which pattern below is like the pattern in the box? (*Circle the correct answer.*)

7	7	7	6	5	7	7	7	6	5

A. 2 2 3 2 2 2 3 2 2 3

B. 5 6 5 6 5 6 5 6 5 6

C. 6 6 6 5 4 6 6 6 5 4

DAILY Warm-Up 46

Name _____ Date _____

1. Look at the table. If 6 is put in the "IN" column, write what would be the number in the "OUT" column.

IN	OUT
2	4
4	8
6	

2. Jimmy bought 10 marbles. Then, he lost some marbles. He now has 4 marbles. How many marbles did Jimmy lose?

_____ marbles

DAILY Warm-Up 47 Name _____ Date _____

1. Which card would be next in the pattern? (*Circle the correct letter.*)

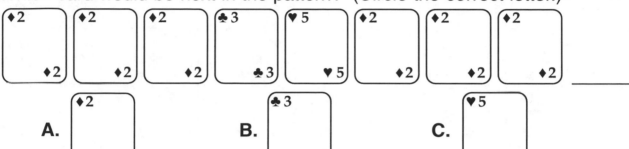

A. **B.** **C.**

2. Circle if the number sentence is *true* or *false*.

$$9 + \boxed{2} = 6 + 4$$

True

False

DAILY Warm-Up 48 Name _____ Date _____

1. Draw what comes next in the pattern.

2. Which card comes next in the pattern? (*Circle the correct letter.*)

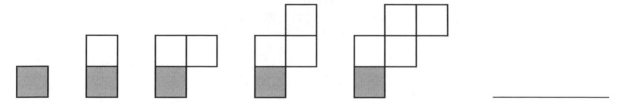

A. **B.** **C.**

DAILY Warm-Up 49

Name _____ **Date** _____

1. Draw the dots on the blank domino that will complete the pattern.

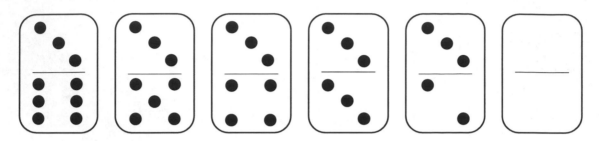

2. Use the numbers 8, 9, and 17 to write four number sentences.

_____ + _____ = _____   _____ − _____ = _____

_____ + _____ = _____   _____ − _____ = _____

DAILY Warm-Up 50

Name _____ **Date** _____

1. Complete each table. Use the example as your guide.

Example

+ 4	
5	9
6	10
7	11

+ 5	
6	
7	
8	

+ 6	
3	
4	
5	

+ 7	
7	
8	
9	

2. Name the pattern.

T t G G d T t G G d

_____

Name _____ **Date** _____

1. Which card would be next in the pattern? *(Circle the correct letter.)*

| ♦2 two ♦2 | ♦3 three ♦3 | ♦3 three ♦3 | ♥4 four ♥4 | ♥4 four ♥4 | ♦2 two ♦2 | ♦3 three ♦3 | ♦3 three ♦3 | ____ |

A. ♦2 two ♦2   **B.** ♦3 three ♦3   **C.** ♥4 four ♥4

2. Name the pattern below.

gAAsgAAs

_____

Name _____ **Date** _____

1. If 7 is put in the "IN" column, what number will be put in the "OUT" column? *(Circle the correct letter.)*

IN	2	3	4	5	6	7
OUT	1	2	3	4	5	

A. 7   **B.** 6   **C.** 8

2. Complete the pattern of numbers in the boxes below.

1	3	5	7		11	13	

Name _____ **Date** _____

1. Find the missing numbers.

$y + 3 = 9$	$12 + y = 16$	$11 + y = 17$
$y =$ _____	$y =$ _____	$y =$ _____

2. Look at the pattern. Circle the letter of the two missing shapes.

 **A.**   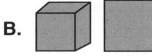 **B.**   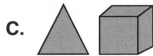 **C.**

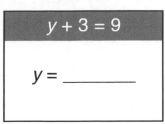

Name _____ **Date** _____

1. Look at the pattern below. Which shape comes next in the pattern? (*Circle the correct letter.*)

 A.

 B.

 C.

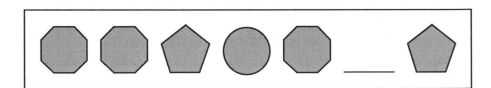

2. Solve the problem.

$$13 + w = 19$$

$$w = \text{_____}$$

Name _____ **Date** _____

Warm-Up 55

1. Look at the table. Add the top number to each number in the left column.
(*The first one is done for you.*)

+ 4	
3	7
5	
7	
9	

2. Write the rule of the table below.

IN	1	2	3	4
OUT	2	3	4	5

What is the rule?

Name _____ **Date** _____

Warm-Up 56

1. Solve the problem.

$$6 + \boxed{} = 3 + 7$$

2. Draw the triangles in the 5th pattern.

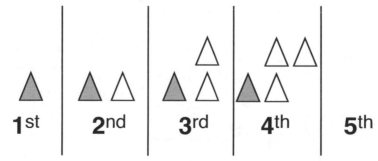

1st　　**2**nd　　**3**rd　　**4**th　　**5**th

Name _____ **Date** _____

1. Solve the problem.

$$3 + 6 = 2 + \boxed{}$$

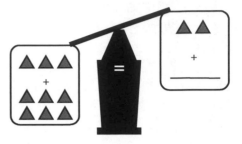

What missing number will balance the scale?

2. Solve the problem.

$$\boxed{} + 4 = 6 + 3$$

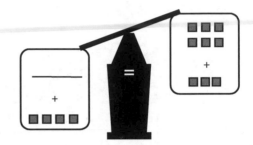

What missing number will balance the scale?

Name _____ **Date** _____

1. Solve the problem.

$$3 + 7 = \boxed{} + 2$$

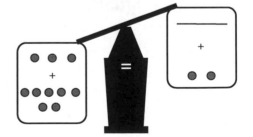

What missing number will balance the scale?

2. What number is missing in the pattern? (*Circle the correct letter.*)

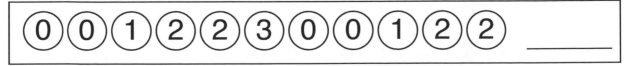

A. (0) **B.** (1) **C.** (3)

DAILY Warm-Up 59   Name _____   Date _____

1. Look at the pattern. Color the empty circle to continue the pattern.

Color **O** circles orange.

Color **B** circles blue.

2. Draw the dots on the blank domino that will complete the pattern.

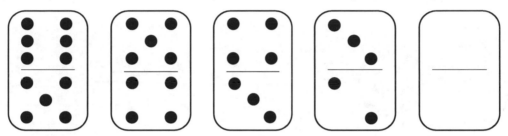

- -

DAILY Warm-Up 60   Name _____   Date _____

1. Write the number that is missing in the pattern.

3,   6,   ____,   12,   15

2. Continue the pattern.

1, 1, 2, 2, 3, 3, 4, 4, 5, 5, 6, ____

DAILY Warm-Up 61   **Name** _____   **Date** _____

1. Which card would be next in the pattern? (*Circle the correct letter.*)

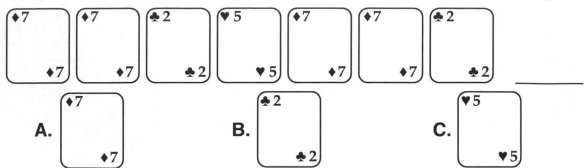

A.   B.   C.

2. Which pattern is this? (*Circle the correct letter.*)

A. ABBBCD

B. ABCDAB

C. ABBCDA

DAILY Warm-Up 62   **Name** _____   **Date** _____

1. How many triangles are there in all?

_____ triangles

2. Write four number sentences for the number 12, 5, and 7.

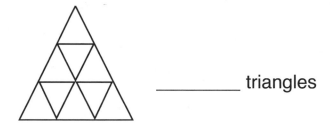

_____ + _____ = _____   _____ − _____ = _____

_____ + _____ = _____   _____ − _____ = _____

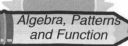
Warm-Up 1

1.

+3		+2	
2	5	3	5
3	6	4	6
4	7	5	7
5	8	6	8

2. 8, 10, 12

Warm-Up 2

1. B   2. D

Warm-Up 3

1. A = 15, 18   2. B
   B = 2, 1
   C = 25, 30

Warm-Up 4

1. C
2. A =

   B =

Warm-Up 5

1. C   2. B, B

Warm-Up 6

1.

Number of Toes	
1 person = 10 toes	5 people = 50 toes
2 people = 20 toes	6 people = 60 toes
3 people = 30 toes	7 people = 70 toes
4 people = 40 toes	8 people = 80 toes

The pattern is counting by 10s.

2. B

Warm-Up 7

1. A. 2
   B. 0
   C. 2
   D. 3
   E. 1
   F. 1
   G. 1
   H. 2
   I. 2
2. 9

Warm-Up 8

1. 4
2. A. 0   D. 0   G. 1
   B. 0   E. 0   H. 0
   C. 0   F. 1   I. 0

Warm-Up 9

1. B   2. 3

Warm-Up 10

1.   2. A

Warm-Up 11

1.
          2. 2 + 3 = 5
             3 + 2 = 5
             5 − 2 = 3
             5 − 3 = 2

Warm-Up 12

1.

+2		+3		+4	
4	6	5	8	1	5
5	7	6	9	2	6
6	8	7	10	3	7

2. AABCAABC

Warm-Up 13

1. 0   2. 3

Warm-Up 14

1. 1   2. B

Warm-Up 15

1.

2. 2 + 6 = 8
   6 + 2 = 8
   8 − 2 = 6
   8 − 6 = 2

Warm-Up 16

1. AABCAABC
2. Answers will vary.

Warm-Up 17

1. 52, 62, 72   2. +3, −1

Warm-Up 18

1.   2. B

Warm-Up 19

1. $y = 4$
2. 9 + 5 = 14   14 − 9 = 5
   5 + 9 = 14   14 − 5 = 9

Warm-Up 20

1. 7, 6   2. 0

Warm-Up 21

1. 6   2. 7

Warm-Up 22

1. 7   2. A

Warm-Up 23

1. 6 + 2 = 8   2. 2
   2 + 6 = 8
   8 − 2 = 6
   8 − 6 = 2

Warm-Up 24

1. 4 + 3 = 7   2. The number 1
   3 + 4 = 7   is being added
   7 − 3 = 4   to the "IN"
   7 − 4 = 3   numbers.

Warm-Up 25

1. B   2. 8

Warm-Up 26

1. B   2. 10, 16

Warm-Up 27

1. 8, 10
2.

Warm-Up 28

1. B   2. 7

Warm-Up 29

1. 8   2. B

Warm-Up 30

1. A   2. 9

Warm-Up 31

1. The last circle should be colored yellow.

2.

Warm-Up 32

1. 14
2. F

Algebra, Patterns and Function

Answer Key

Warm-Up 33
1. 6   2. 7

Warm-Up 34
1. 8
   4
2. False
   False

Warm-Up 35
1. A   2. B

Warm-Up 36
1. 8   2. 7

Warm-Up 37
1. The pattern is counting by 2s.
2. B

Warm-Up 38
1.

2. C

Warm-Up 39
1. 30, 35, 40
2. 13, 21, 27, 35

Warm-Up 40
1. 20, 24
2. 11, 23

Warm-Up 41
1. C
2. $4 + 5 = 9$
   $5 + 4 = 9$
   $9 - 5 = 4$
   $9 - 4 = 5$

Warm-Up 42
1. A. 7
   B. 0
   C. 5
   D. 6
2. C

Warm-Up 43
1. 12
2. B

Warm-Up 44
1. A
2. A. 1   C. 9   E. 11
   B. 6   D. 4   F. 7

Warm-Up 45
1. 15   2. C

Warm-Up 46
1. 12   2. 6

Warm-Up 47
1. B
2. False

Warm-Up 48
1.

2. A

Warm-Up 49
1.   2. $8 + 9 = 17$
                   $9 + 8 = 17$
                   $17 - 8 = 9$
                   $17 - 9 = 8$

Warm-Up 50
1.

+ 5		+ 6		+ 7	
6	11	3	9	7	14
7	12	4	10	8	15
8	13	5	11	9	16

2. ABCCDABCCD

Warm-Up 51
1. C
2. ABBCABBC

Warm-Up 52
1. B
2. 9, 15

Warm-Up 53
1. $y = 6$ $y = 4$ $y = 6$
2. B

Warm-Up 54
1. A
2. $w = 6$

Warm-Up 55
1.

+4	
3	7
5	9
7	11
9	13

2. +1

Warm-Up 56
1. 4
2.

Warm-Up 57
1. 7
2. 5

Warm-Up 58
1. 8
2. C

Warm-Up 59
1. The circle should be colored blue.
2.

Warm-Up 60
1. 9
2. 6

Warm-Up 61
1. C
2. C

Warm-Up 62
1. 13
2. $5 + 7 = 12$
   $7 + 5 = 12$
   $12 - 5 = 7$
   $12 - 7 = 5$